"Larry Weidel is a leader with the ability to be both personally successful and reproduce that success in others. It is a rare skill; very few people can do both. In Serial Winner, Larry shares his unique vision and pairs it with the actions you need to take to win over and over again in business and in life."

— **Glenn Williams**, CEO of Primerica

"Success in life and business always requires a multistep formula of discovery and integration. Larry Weidel's experiences in business have resulted in a playbook of tips and tricks as he characterizes and defines the common traits of the serial winner. The serial winner is a finisher that is omnipresent, humble, always self-aware, and emotionally intelligent. This winner is also a leader and a team player that is constantly optimistic, self-improving, and growing. In addition the focus, the ability to do grunt work with perseverance, and the willingness to adapt to change are the hallmark exemplary features of this successful individual. This book challenges us to discover that the win is always within each of us waiting to be mastered!"

—**Bert R. Mandelbaum**, MD, author of
The Win Within: Capturing Your Victorious Spirit

"For over a decade, Larry has been an invaluable mentor who has pushed me to achieve repeated success. *Serial Winner* captures Larry's key teachings and presents the ideas in terms that anyone can understand and apply to all endeavors. All you need to succeed are the desire to be your best and Larry's five actions!"

—**John Clendenin**, US Ski Hall of Fame member and founder of the Clendenin Method

"*Serial Winner* will teach you to cultivate habits that will help you build a winner's attitude. Each chapter is full of tips and anecdotes that will inspire you to be more committed to your goals and embrace the perseverance to reach them."

—**Todd Mullins**, lead pastor, Christ Fellowship

"There's a saying that goes, 'You are what you eat and the company you keep.' Larry Weidel is definitely great company. He has proven to be wise and resourceful in his approach to success. *Serial Winner* is an eye-opening tool for anyone needing guidance and motivation for next-level thinking. If you like winning as much as I do, this is for you."

—**Lee Haney**, 8-time Mr. Olympia, past chairman to the President's Council on Fitness, founder of the International Association of Fitness Sciences

SERIAL
WINNER

SERIAL
WINNER

5 ACTIONS TO CREATE YOUR CYCLE OF SUCCESS

LARRY WEIDEL

GREENLEAF
BOOK GROUP PRESS

This publication is designed to provide accurate and authoritative information in regard to the subject matter covered. It is sold with the understanding that the publisher and author are not engaged in rendering professional services. If expert assistance is required, the services of a competent professional should be sought.

References to A.L. Williams (now Primerica) are historical in nature. Primerica offers a tremendous opportunity for individuals who work hard and who desire to develop a business with strong income potential.

Published by Greenleaf Book Group Press
Austin, Texas
www.gbgpress.com

Distributed by Greenleaf Book Group

For ordering information or special discounts for bulk purchases, please contact Greenleaf Book Group at PO Box 91869, Austin, TX 78709, 512-891-6100.

Design and composition by Greenleaf Book Group
Cover design by Greenleaf Book Group
Cover images: ©iStockphoto.com/seamartini

Publisher's Cataloging-in-Publication Data is available.

ISBN: 978-1-62634-234-7

TreeNeutral

Part of the Tree Neutral® program, which offsets the number of trees consumed in the production and printing of this book by taking proactive steps, such as planting trees in direct proportion to the number of trees used: www.treeneutral.com

Printed in the United States of America on acid-free paper

15 16 17 18 19 20   10 9 8 7 6 5 4 3 2 1

First Edition

Other Edition(s):
eBook ISBN: 978-1-62634-235-4

For my parents,

Andrew J. Weidel and Mary O. Weidel

CONTENTS

THE CYCLE OF WINNING

We all know people in life who seem to move from success to success, with barely a pause or dip in between. They're always talking about their next big project or goal. They're always excited about *something*. They have limitless energy, which they use to accomplish more and more. They are role models and opinion-makers. They always seem ahead of the game. They stay on their feet. They lead rewarding lives.

They are serial winners. In a world full of people who almost win, they are the few who do it again and again.

To most of us, serial winners are confounding. They seem to have the ability to shed the negatives in life and attract the positives. How do they find the energy or time? we ask. How did they get there so fast? How do they fit it all in? We just don't understand how these people achieve what they do. Because for the most part, they don't seem all that special. Many of them started where we did. Sure, some had elite training, but most didn't have any extra advantages (and some had even fewer)—they worked their way up from the streets. (Did you know that most millionaires in the United States are first-generation or self-made?)

So we try to follow their moves. We study what they say. We may stick some of their better quotes on the wall. We even copy their style—how they dress, their mannerisms, their haircuts. They become our models. Why? Because we want similar things. We want opportunities. We want to contribute to our communities. We want to lead fulfilling lives. We want to have fun! We want to do big things. Yet we still seem to be missing some important piece.

That piece is *action*—consistent action that leads to consistent progress.

Serial winners leverage a cycle of *winning action* to make progress. They *do something* every day that puts them or keeps them on course for the things they want in life. Along the way, they steadily overcome friction and other forces that could slow them down or knock them off course. By focusing on what they can and should do, they manage themselves out of tough, demoralizing situations. The result? They are always moving forward, following their passions, having fun, and contributing to the world.

What about you? Are you achieving everything you want to achieve? Are you making the progress you would like, or do you feel stuck? Do you have an itch to break out, try something new, or go for more? Is there something great you want to make happen in your career, your life, or even the world? If you're okay with your life remaining exactly as it is now, this book probably isn't for you. But if you can picture yourself doing more and doing bigger, this book can help. Because the only difference between you and a serial winner is five basic actions.

And there is nothing keeping you from applying those five actions in your own life.

THERE'S NO PATENT ON ACTION

Even though it may not seem to be true, everybody has won and lost. No one has a perfect batting average, and no one has struck out every single time. Anybody who tells you different is trying to sell you something, so be sure to read the disclaimers. Serial winners bounce back, move on, and win anyway. And they do it through action.

I've had big successes, but I also had to accept food stamps for a time just to keep my wife and two young boys from going hungry. Today I'm a multimillionaire, but I once had a boss label me Turkey of the Month in a company-wide newsletter (no kidding). I know what it is to have nothing go right, to be passed over for promotions, to be the one applauding others who were getting ahead. But I've learned a lot about success and winning along the way. And I have spent the past forty years building a national financial services organization and helping the many, many people on my team achieve the success they want. Hundreds have been able to earn six-figure annual incomes, and even more have earned the label "millionaire." I had to dig harder and longer than some people, but when it takes you longer, you value the results and what you learned along the way more.

When I started my career, everything was hard. But my weaknesses gave me an edge. I knew I didn't have a chance of making something great out of my life unless I paid attention. I studied the winners I knew closely. I asked *a lot* of questions. (I'm surprised people didn't start walking the other way when they saw me coming.) And I figured out what I had to do— step by step, detail by detail—to improve. I caught on to the fact that the people who were winning weren't better than me. They simply *did things that I wasn't doing*.

I learned something important: nothing can keep us from doing what winners do. There's no copyright on wisdom, and there's no patent on action.

My biggest advantage has been the incredible circle of advisors and mentors in my life. I learned about coaching from "Bullet Bob" Turley, professional pitcher and winner of the Cy Young Award. My cousin, Edward Roberts, who was known as "the father of the personal computer," taught me how to follow my curiosity and apply my drive. Art Williams, founder of the A.L. Williams & Associates life insurance company (now Primerica), taught me a lot about how to be a winning leader.

Everything I've achieved, I've achieved by watching the best. How do the best do it? How did they get to the top and how do they stay on top? I wasn't interested in modeling just anyone. I wanted to watch what the top people did, because obviously they knew and did things that most people didn't. Life is too short to figure everything out on your own.

Unfortunately, not enough people have access to great mentors and coaches. They aren't close enough to serial winners to spot the simple pattern they all apply. And that is why I wrote this book—to help people discover the patterns that could catapult them to a new level of success and happiness.

THE CYCLE OF WINNING

Over the years, I figured out the go-to moves—the cycle of action that winners use to achieve what they want. The winners who return to this cycle again and again, day after day, have serial success. These five actions get them on track and help them stay on track. What are they?

- **Decide**

- **Overdo**

- **Adjust**

- **Finish**

- **Improve**

It's true, these concepts aren't complicated. But the greats from every walk of life talk about using them to win. So why don't more people win? Because most people don't really understand them, don't apply them, or don't apply them consistently. "Yeah, yeah, I know," they say. But what they believe is that these actions seem too simple to be important. There must be something more to it, right? So they keep looking for a more complicated answer that doesn't exist, ignoring the valuable answer they've already been given.

Here's the bottom line: Anyone who wants more out of life and is frustrated enough to do something about it can learn and apply what winners do. Winners keep things simple. And where winners always start is with these fundamentals. So if you ever find yourself asking, "Who says I have to sit on the sidelines? Who says I have to live on the leftovers of people who are doing the things I would like to do?" this is where you should start, too.

WINNING ISN'T A ONE-TIME THING

Will Rogers once said, "Even if you are on the right track, you'll get run over if you just sit there." You may be a hard worker. You may have a great attitude. (In fact, I'm pretty sure these sentences describe you because lazy, negative people don't buy books like this.) But to win in life, you have to keep making progress. Winning isn't a one-time thing.

Unfortunately, when some force has come along and

knocked us off our path, we can become confused. We don't have a clue as to what to do next, so many of us stop doing anything. We sit there.

What I will help you discover is practical answers to the most basic of all questions: "So *now* what do I do?" The answer is, "Turn to the fundamentals. Go back to the basics." The cycle of winning can always guide us to appropriate action. It shapes how winners respond to whatever life throws at them.

If you are struggling to choose a path and start down it, I'll explain how to decide on a goal or destination and commit to it. If you've started down a new path but don't seem to be making much progress, I'll show you how to build momentum. If you have hit a hurdle that is stopping you in your tracks, I'll share the methods that all winners use to adjust and keep going. Most important, I'll help you keep yourself from quitting when you are moments away from winning. And then I'll describe how to keep going—on to the next and bigger thing. What I will come back to again and again is the importance of *doing*.

If things aren't happening for you right now, there's something you can do about it. And it's probably one of the five fundamentals I'll cover in this book. As you read, you'll realize that you're already doing some of these things. But one or more of them will jump out at you—the things you're missing. It's like a Ferrari with a bad spark plug. Switch it out and you'll be covering ground fast. Stop talking about what you want; stop thinking about what is holding you back. Instead, turn your frustrations and desires into actions. The discipline of consistent action is what self-management is all about. It's the only way to win and keep winning.

I want to get you excited about what's possible and to show you how easy it can be to achieve what you want faster by digging deep on the fundamentals. My mission is to launch a revolution of doing, to unleash an army of people who are ready to race forward toward the great big things they *really* want to do—that they are destined to do.

If you're ready to join that army, read on.

THE **CYCLE** OF **WINNING**

1 DECIDE

2 OVERDO

3 ADJUST

4 FINISH

5 KEEP IMPROVING

CHAPTER 1

DON'T HESITATE, DECIDE

In football, the clock is always ticking.

You're the coach, and the game is going to be over before you know it. You'll probably run seventy-five offensive plays, and every single one of them is designed to score a touchdown. If you're lucky, maybe three or four of them will result in points on the board. But at any moment in the game, you call the play that you think is the best option. If it doesn't work out the way you wanted, at least you have more information when choosing the next one. And maybe you're in a better position. No matter what, you don't waste time hesitating or debating. *You keep calling plays and you keep moving down the field.*

Art Williams used to tell me this all the time. It has a powerful message behind it that has always stuck with me:

If you want to win, you have to keep moving forward. To keep moving forward, you have to keep making decisions.

Unfortunately, too many people who have the urge to do big things get stuck somewhere along the way. Some people get stuck early. For others it happens later in life. Maybe somebody convinced them they simply aren't good enough. Maybe nobody was around to show them how to take the next step. Maybe something went wrong and they can't seem to figure out what to do next. Whatever the reason, they lose their nerve. Doubt takes over and they hesitate, they lose time, they get farther behind. They become convinced that they don't have what it takes to win or they lose touch with what it is they

Decide or Drift.
Either Way, the Clock Is Ticking.

really want. Eventually, they stop making decisions that will move them forward. They stop *trying*.

Serial winners don't let little, limiting things like doubt and uncertainty stand in their way. Lack of advantage doesn't matter. The people who say, "You can't" don't matter. They focus more on what they want than on why they can't have it, and then they decide to do what it takes to get it. Then they dive in. They see something they want—a promotion or two or three, a new career, their own business—and they make the big decision to go for it. Then they make smaller decisions every day that keep them moving toward the goal, and the next one, and the next one.

WINNERS CONQUER DOUBT

—

The three killers of dreams are detail-itis, excuse-itis,
and the hesitation virus. And they all stem from doubt.

Not one of us is free of it. We all have moments when we question our ability to succeed and our ability to make good decisions. Why? Because we can't know the future. Winners feel doubt just as often as anybody else. They understand you have to earn success. They know you can't be haphazard if you want to make progress toward your most important goals. These truths inevitably lead to questions about their ability to succeed.

If we aren't on guard, though, those moments can expand and can kill our spirit. They can demoralize. They can give us a faulty perspective. They can distract us and disrupt our forward momentum. They can waste our precious time. The clock is ticking and you can spend your time worrying and doubting or you can spend your time working.

When you allow doubt to send you into a tailspin of indecision and hesitation, you invite fear. You grind to a halt. All work stops, and with no work, you have no hope.

With fear comes paralysis, and with paralysis comes certain failure.

When winners feel doubt, they manage themselves—as fast as possible—away from the overwhelming tendency to hesitate, overthink, and overanalyze. They combat doubt with decision that drives positive action. They take the next step as quickly as possible, whatever it is. Serial winners know that the worst thing you can do is to let yourself get frustrated, confused, and stalled out. They do allow themselves to question, however, because finding out the facts helps them set a definite path. Galileo said, "All truths are easy to understand once they are discovered; the point is to discover them." Confusion is the beginning of clarity. This is how progress is made in the world and this is how progress is made in our lives.

The decisions we make and the actions we take are how we create the life we want. You're either living the life you create for yourself or you're living the life that other people create for you, with their decisions and actions. It's your life. You have to live it. It might as well be the one you choose.

Throughout the rest of the chapters, I'll explore different sources of doubt that can blindside us. But if you feel stalled out or stuck right now, a good first step to getting going again is to take a close look at your fundamental beliefs about what's possible.

BREAKING OUT OF THE COCOON

When I was growing up, we moved every year because my father was in the military. By the time I was twenty-one we had moved twenty-seven times and I had gone to twelve schools in four different states and three different countries. Eventually, I was old enough to notice that the people in each place we lived had their own views about the world. Sometimes those views were very different. And even as a kid I knew that sometimes those views were just not accurate—because I had already been exposed to quite a bit of the world. Many of the people I met had not. They lived in a cocoon.

Whether you recognize it or not, you probably live in a cocoon, too—or did at some point. We all have.

The cocoon starts with the protected environment in which we grow up. It's constructed of opinions, values, beliefs, and priorities. We absorb them from our parents and the few adults we encounter in our early formative years. Within this cocoon, we learn what's right and what's wrong, who we trust and who we don't, what's important and what isn't, where we belong and where we don't, and most important, what's possible and what isn't. The people in our lives—family, teachers, community—create that cocoon based on what they've been told and what they've experienced. These attitudes and beliefs are embedded deep in our core as we grow up. Even if we grow up to be very different from our parents or other adults in our community, we've been influenced by them in a thousand little ways. We often don't even realize how much so.

Now, your cocoon might be made up of encouraging beliefs, like "Anything is possible if you want it badly enough" and "You've got what it takes to succeed." But from what I've seen and from the people I've met, that's not the case most of the time. I would bet that some of the beliefs that make up your cocoon aren't doing you any good. They are limiting. They convince you that statements like "I don't have what it takes" or "Things like that don't happen to people like me" are true. These are just lies we have internalized, based on myths about what it takes to win in life.

Not sure you believe in the power of the cocoon? Take a look at the research done on how what we believe affects our performance, our ability to learn, and so many other things. Carol Dweck, author of the popular book *Mindset: The New Psychology of Success* (Random House, 2006) conducted a study with middle-school students with lousy math grades. One group was taught study skills. The other group was taught the same skills *and* the idea of the "malleability of intelligence"—they were told they had the ability to get better at math because they could grow their intelligence and get smarter.[1] Which group do you think got better at math? The second group. Why? Because they believed they could! Somebody shared *facts* that helped them conquer their doubt. The truth is that the biggest factor in what we achieve is what we believe we're capable of achieving.

Our cocoons have the power to influence us—unless they are challenged. It doesn't matter where your cocoon came from or what it looks like. Until you break out of it, you'll have a hard time fulfilling your potential. People who do break out either are forced out by the things they experience or fight their way out. Let me help you make a dent by breaking down some of the myths that exist in most cocoons.

The Myths of Advantage

Misinformation about what makes some people successful and others not seems unavoidable. Depending on where we came from and the experiences of our family and friends, we've been bombarded by any number of myths about winning. They hang out in our subconscious and influence our thought processes and our actions.

Even though everybody's cocoon is different, most of us share certain myths. The most common and debilitating are the myths of advantage:

- **Myth #1: Winners are just born that way.**
  Let's talk about the people who start life with every advantage. You know who they are. They're smarter. They learn faster. They're naturally talented in sports or music or computer programming. They have sparkling, magnetic personalities. They stand out in a crowd. Studies have shown that people who are better looking, people who are taller, and people who have higher IQs generally make more money. They are born to win, and if you aren't one of them, you'll always be runner up.

- **Myth #2: Winners come from better families.**
  People from better families are destined to succeed, of course. They grow up with loving parents who have good jobs. They live in the right neighborhoods. Their parents never criticize or belittle them. Instead, they support them in all their endeavors, encouraging them to study, to compete, to be the best they can be. If they need extra coaching or special equipment to improve, you can bet it's available.

  A better family usually means a better network of well-connected friends and relations who are happy to help these people get ahead. Grandparents, uncles, aunts, cousins, neighbors—everyone wants and expects them to win. People from better families grow up safe and secure, knowing they'll never have to "go it alone." They are so well loved, well coached, and well cared for by their family and friends that they have no fear of the future. They are ready to step into their roles as guaranteed winners. The road to the top is paved for them in advance.

- **Myth #3: Winners are better educated.**
  Education creates an unbeatable advantage. All winners are in part successful because they graduate with important degrees, usually from the best schools. They've benefited immeasurably from specialized, elite training that most people only dream of. Their superior education allows them to think on a higher level. They know how to strategize. They never run out of ideas. They're incredible problem-solvers and leaders, with the ability to organize and run huge projects.

  Their formal education has allowed them to meet and develop relationships with experts—mentors who took extra time and care to reveal all the secrets of success. When problems arise, this network of experts can be called upon to deliver the right answers right away. As a result, winners almost never get stuck.

So what do you do if you don't fit the winner's mold? What if you aren't naturally gifted? What if you don't have a great, supportive family and a spectacular, high-dollar education? You should give up! It's pointless to compete with people who are sure to get the best positions, the best opportunities, and the lion's share of support. Unlike you, they won't have to experience the pain of a slow start or the disgrace of failure.

Does this sound like BS? Of course it does! And yet on some level, *most of us believe it.* We live in a cocoon of belief that our disadvantages will prevent us from creating the life we want.

Here's the truth:

> ## *No advantage is a guarantee that you'll win. No lack of advantage is a guarantee that you'll lose.*

Bust the Myths

It's up to each of us to overcome our particular circumstances and to make the most of what we're given. No myth about winning can stand up to that truth. As Calvin Coolidge once said, "Nothing in this world can take the place of persistence. Talent will not; nothing is more common than unsuccessful people with talent. Genius will not; unrewarded genius is almost a proverb. Education will not; the world is full of educated derelicts. Persistence and determination alone are omnipotent."

Everybody is born blessed with some level of talent and ability. Those natural advantages can certainly help you win—but only if you're willing to develop them and put them to work for you.

Unfortunately, that's often not what happens. Sometimes too much of a good thing can backfire. Being gifted can make life difficult. Gifted athletes may struggle to prove they aren't "dumb jocks." Geniuses can struggle to relate to other people. Most of us assume that really beautiful people aren't very intelligent. (How surprised are you when you find out that a model attends an Ivy League college?) And being naturally good at something can make it difficult to learn the pattern of hard work necessary to reach elite levels.

Likewise, having a supportive family can give you a strong foundation, but parents can only drive you so far in life. Eventually you have to take the wheel. And while privileged children may get lots of attention, many times it's of the wrong kind. They grow up with unrealistic expectations for themselves, piled on top of unrealistic expectations from those around them. They may be pressured into activities and even careers for which they have no passion or aptitude. That pressure can cause them to burn out early. Growing up in a wealthy family can breed even more challenges: an entitlement attitude, poor financial judgment, an inability to connect fulfillment with contribution to the world. Why do you think Warren Buffett plans to give away 99 percent of his wealth before or after he dies? He has famously said, "I want to give my kids just enough so that they would feel that they could do anything, but not so much that they would feel like doing nothing." Whatever the circumstances, no family or upbringing is perfect.

An education can be a valuable thing, it's true. But as someone with a degree from both a four-year college and the school of hard knocks, I can tell you that there are many things you need to learn about how to succeed that the best colleges in the world will never teach you. People don't get an automatic pass into the boardroom just because they graduated from Harvard. Degrees give you credentials, but they don't necessarily do anything for your character, coach-ability, and commitment—which play huge roles in your ability to achieve. A college education is only a start. I'm proud to be a graduate of Georgia Tech, but I know that your most valuable education happens outside of the classroom, and usually begins after you receive your degree.

If you're feeling undereducated, it might be helpful to know how many people have done big things without a college degree, or even a high-school degree in some cases. Here's a short list: Bill Gates, Paul Allen, Steve Jobs, Steve Wozniak, Ray Kroc, Walt Disney, Annie Leibovitz, Wolfgang Puck, Ellen DeGeneres, Richard Branson, Kelly Clarkson, Mark Zuckerberg, Glenn Beck, Cindy Crawford, Carl Bernstein, Paula Deen, Andrew Carnegie, Winston Churchill, Michael Dell, Ted Turner, David Geffen, and Larry Ellison, to name just a few. Most of these people are millionaires and quite a few are billionaires. And many are doing big, world-changing things with their money.

The Disadvantage of Advantage

The biggest disadvantage of an early advantage is that growing up in a "perfect" world can make you soft.

I think this is why Henry David Thoreau wrote, "It is the greatest of all advantages to enjoy no advantage at all." When you've had it easy, it's hard to adjust when things start to get a little tough. If you grow up without learning how to overcome obstacles on your own, you might not recover when you suffer your first failure. And you will fail. Everybody does. Winners are the ones who know how to keep moving forward anyway.

William Deresiewicz, who was a Yale professor for ten years, wrote a book titled *Excellent Sheep* (Free Press, 2014) that makes similar points. The most privileged students at the best colleges aren't being taught to think and don't understand how to create meaningful lives:

> The system manufactures students who are smart and talented and driven, yes, but also anxious, timid, and lost, with little intellectual curiosity and a stunted sense of purpose: trapped in a bubble of privilege, heading meekly in the same direction, great at what they're doing but with no idea why they're doing it.[2]

Deresiewicz makes strong points, but I don't think he uses the word "driven" correctly. The people he's describing are going through the motions, doing what's expected of them.

Granted, those expectations are high and meeting those expectations takes hard work, but that's not drive. That's being bullied into pursuing a life you aren't even sure you want.

By comparison, disadvantages are often the source of drive and determination. You've heard the old cliché, "It's not the size of the dog in the fight; it's the size of the fight in the dog." It's true. Millions are born with advantages and never learn how to leverage them.

> *Every day, people with fewer advantages and more drive decide to outthink, outwork, and outperform their more "advantaged" counterparts.*

Check out the most-valuable-player award winners on high-school, college, or even pro teams. They often aren't the most gifted players. Invariably, they *are* among the most committed and driven.

Whether you have passion or talent or some other advantage, it's meaningless until you do something with it. In the Parable of the Talents (Matthew 25:14–30), the Lord sends a message: doing nothing with the resources we're given because we fear the possible outcome is offensive. Why? Because that's not how we contribute to the world or lead meaningful lives.

YOU OWE IT TO YOURSELF TO GET THE FACTS

I played just about any sport I could when I was in school—football, basketball, baseball, tennis, even track and field. I was never the best athlete, but I always made the team. Why? My father was in the US Air Force, and I was often in schools on military bases or in towns nearby. The schools were usually small, which meant you had a good shot at getting on just about any team if you tried out. So I was exposed to lots of teams and lots of coaches in lots of towns.

When I look back on it, it's amazing to me the lack of vision of the coaches I played for—people responsible for coaching, teaching, and inspiring young athletes. None of them had any vision other than getting ready for the next game or match. I don't remember starting a single season with an inspiring speech about winning the championship. I never heard them talk about making extra effort in order to make the all-star team. They never talked about other players they had coached who had gotten sports scholarships. Maybe they had limited views of their own abilities. They were in their own cocoon. Because of this, they couldn't envision anything greater for the athletes.

Some of the people I played with were really good. They had elite-level talent. I don't know if they were cut out for the pros, but they definitely could have received college scholarships if they had put in a little extra effort. Unfortunately, nobody ever told them that was a possibility. Sure, we had a general sense that the team could get a bit better through practice. But nobody ever sat us down and said, "If you really want to improve, if you want to try for a scholarship, here's what you can do." We never talked about clinics. We never talked about special coaching to build certain skills. We never talked about off-season camps. No one challenged us to look higher, to shoot for bigger things. Amazingly, no one mentioned the possibility of becoming an all-star or getting a college scholarship. So none of us considered these opportunities or put in the kind of effort necessary to make them happen.

The truth is that at the professional level of every major sport, you'll find players who came from small towns and small teams with poor facilities. Often, a coach, a parent, or another adult made the difference by pushing the athlete to go for something bigger. They got scholarships, they became all-stars, they got drafted. If you read the stories of some of the football greats, you'll find out that a lot of them worked hard just to make it onto the third string of their college teams. Success didn't come easily, and early on they didn't look that special to most people. But because of their drive to improve and the belief that they had a chance to succeed, they became special. Often you'll hear them say that it all started when someone saw potential in them and challenged them to go for greatness.

Look at Kurt Warner—he wasn't even drafted by the NFL out of college. In fact, he couldn't even get a Division I college to give him a scholarship. But he never lost his grip on his dream of playing in the pros. It took him a while. He had to attend a Division II school, play in the Arena Football League, bag groceries at $5.50 an hour to survive, and then play in NFL Europe before he got his chance. But once he did, he made an impact. In his second year he quarterbacked the St. Louis Rams to victory in the Super Bowl, winning the game's MVP award in the process!

Just because somebody tells you something can't be done doesn't mean that it can't. Just because somebody never tells you you're good enough or capable enough to make something happen doesn't mean you aren't. It simply means that they don't know how to do it. Why do we have the word "pioneer" in our language? Because we need a term for all the people who do things that nobody else has ever done. And they are everywhere.

I knew a woman who wanted to become an editor at a publishing company. Apparently, it's tough to get in on the editorial side of the business. The competition is fierce. Even though she was told that getting a job in a non-editorial department would never lead her to an editorial position—it would only put her on track for promotions in that department—she took a job in production. She kept signing up for cross-department groups, offered editorial advice on her projects when it seemed appropriate, developed positive relationships with the editors, and eventually, she got a job in editorial. She couldn't believe all the email she received from others in production offering congratulations and asking how she had made the leap.

What beliefs about what is possible and what is not run rampant in your company? Are you letting them hold you back?

It's easy to fall into the trap of believing what we're told by people who seem to know better or who seem to have our best interests at heart. We usually don't consider that there is more they *aren't* telling us, usually because they don't know. The people teaching or guiding us frequently only have the opportunity to study winners from afar; they never get past the superficial "packaging." What winning looks like from the outside is advantages and luck. From the perspective of families or communities or groups where few people break out and do something big, this is especially true. Their assumptions about winning are wrong—they never learn what makes true winners tick. Incorrect assumptions based on incomplete evidence are the source of the myths we believe and of our own doubts.

Instead of accepting the myths and doubts, winners challenge them. They don't meekly accept that they don't have a chance. *They don't let themselves be bullied into not trying.* They dig in and find out for themselves if what they're being told is true. They find out if the obstacles they're facing are big enough to make trying a waste of time. Usually they find out that lots of people facing the same obstacles win anyway.

Take a look at what it is you believe about success and try to figure out who planted those ideas. Were those people winners? Did they achieve what they wanted in life? If not, should you trust that what they've told you about winning is true?

Conquering doubt means finding your own answers to the questions you have about how to succeed and then developing faith that you'll find a way to make it happen.

WHAT DO YOU WANT AND HOW BAD DO YOU WANT IT?

—

*To people who are just moving through life, punching
the clock and unexcited, running across someone
who is energized and passionate can be jarring.*

They'll wonder, why is he acting like such a maniac? Don't worry. Being called a "maniac" can be good thing. Here's why. Maniacs are driven. They'll do whatever it takes to achieve what they want to achieve. They don't ask, am I good enough? Do I have what it takes? Their internal motivation drives them right past those doubts.

The only questions that matter to winners are Do I really want it? Does it excite me?

It's almost impossible to pick winners out of a crowd because what makes them great is what is inside their minds and hearts. They are monomaniacs on a mission. Sometimes you can see it in their eyes. They want it more than everyone else. And they do what's necessary to give themselves the best chance to make it happen.

Take my cousin Ed as an example. He and I spent summers together on my grandparents' farm when we were kids, and he was a massive source of inspiration for me over the years.

From the beginning, Ed was an inventor. In high school, he had a passion for two things: electronics and medicine. He was always tinkering and inventing—he even built a very simple computer. But what he really wanted was to become a doctor. He spent so much time volunteering and working at the local hospital and became so knowledgeable that the nurses called him Dr. Roberts.

When he graduated, he enrolled in college to study medicine. A neurosurgeon he met, who was also interested in electronics, suggested that he change his major to electrical engineering. He wouldn't be able to study it once he entered medical school. Ed followed his advice and continued to take his pre-med courses too. By his junior year, though, he was married and had a child on the way (this was 1962). He couldn't work part-time, pay for school, and support his family.

Ed wasn't going to let lack of funds stop him, though. He enrolled in the US Air Force to take advantage of the Airman Education and Commissioning Program. It took three years, but in 1965 they sent him to Oklahoma State University to finish his degree.

Now, Ed already had a couple of years of college under his belt, so he should have been able to finish in two years or so. But he wasn't about to waste this opportunity. The Air Force wouldn't pay his way through medical school, but they would have to forcibly remove him from OSU. Since he couldn't pursue medicine, he went full steam ahead toward science. He spent four years there taking every science class he could. He would complete almost all the courses in an area of study, leaving one class undone to avoid graduating. Finally, the Air Force caught on and told him he had to finish. Officially, he graduated with a degree in electrical engineering, but in his final semester, he took all the courses he needed to fulfill about five other majors.

After college, he was assigned to Kirtland Air Force Base in Albuquerque to fulfill his military obligation. He worked with civilian contractors who were building new technology for the Air Force. It was his job to inspect, negotiate, and troubleshoot. He was circulating with contractors who were supplying micro-technology for weapons programs, and that inspired a few ideas.

Ed's backyard hobby was model rockets. Simple rockets weren't enough for him, of course. He started using the new technology to build components for his rockets, like a tiny camera that would take pictures during flight. Within a few years, he had started a side business called Micro Instrumentation and Telemetry Systems (MITS) with a partner. Remember the "micro" part. It becomes important later. They invented and sold model-rocket parts. Eventually, Ed had an idea that the advances in microtechnology could help him put together a build-it-yourself kit for a simple desktop calculator. It was the first American-made desktop calculator, and because of that, it became the cover story for *Popular Electronics*. It was a sensation.

While he was at OSU, Ed had spent a lot of time tinkering around with the university's mainframe, which they let students use. That wasn't good enough for Ed. He eventually built his own mainframe, completely filling up his garage. So when the processors on the market were finally small enough and fast enough, Ed saw an opportunity and seized it. MITS developed a computer—what many people call the first commercially available desktop computer.

The Altair 8800 (some assembly required) was featured on the cover of *Popular Electronics*. From here, you might know the rest of the story. Bill Gates (still at Harvard) and Paul Allen saw that issue and contacted MITS, saying that they had programming language, a BASIC interpreter, that they were certain would work with the Altair 8800. (They hadn't yet written it, however.) Others were calling, too. Ed told Gates and Allen what he told everybody: "The first one to walk through the door with a system that works gets the contract." After a three-week blitz to write the code, Gates and Allen created a functioning system first. In 1975, MITS signed a contract with Allen and Gates and their newly formed company Micro-Soft. You may have heard of it. (I told you "micro" would be important.) The Altair 8800 with BASIC was the first personal computer to be widely available and relatively affordable, at about $400 (which in 1975 was still a bunch of money).

But that isn't the end of the story for Ed. By 1976, sales had exploded and the company was stretched to its limits filling orders. MITS had grown to about 200 employees and Ed's job had evolved into management. He wasn't the most patient soul, and now he was spending all his time on people problems, which held no appeal for him. He was bored. So he decided to sell the company. His share was $2 million. Just $2 million for a computer that would help launch a revolution.

As part of the deal, Ed went to work for the new company designing new products—what he really wanted to do. They set him up as the head of a skunkworks in a little building with a few assistants. He told me that thirty days later, he walked across the parking lot with a working prototype for a laptop computer. The executives looked at him and said, "Who would ever buy this? There's no market for this." At which point Ed said, "Check, please." He realized he was wasting his time and decided to move on.

In late 1977, Ed left New Mexico and bought five farms not far from my grandparents' farm in Georgia. He had spent every summer there growing up, and he decided he would try his hand at farming. In a big way.

Still not the end of the story. In 1982, Mercer University, a well-regarded college in Macon, Georgia, started a medical school. Medicine was Ed's first love, and he immediately signed up to be in the first graduating class. At the age of 45, he graduated from medical school, after a pretty amazing twenty-year detour. He opened a small office in a nearby town and practiced medicine there for seventeen years.

Here's the bottom line of Ed's story:

We can only be great doing things we really want to do, for our own reasons.

I'll admit that there aren't many people in the world like Ed. But we can all learn something from him. If he had sat around feeling sorry for himself when he had to leave college, if he had given up on his dream, all his contributions would have been lost. Instead, he pursued every one of his passions and interests as far as he could—and a lot farther than most.

Amelia Earhart said it well: "I want to do it because I want to do it." When we do things we want to do, we're fueled by a much deeper and stronger drive than we can ever generate when doing things we're forced to do. The hardest thing to do in life is to stay excited. Every job or pursuit comes with tedious work that has to be done. But if it's tied to things we want to be doing or achieving, we find the energy and motivation to push through.

If you don't have a target that motivates you, you'll never find out what's possible. How do you find yours? Start by following your natural curiosity.

FOLLOW YOUR NATURAL CURIOSITY

Ed's advice to me when I went off to college was, "Follow your own natural curiosity. Otherwise, school and business and your job will beat it out of you and you'll just be dull." You want to define your life, not let circumstances define you or send you off on a detour that kills your enthusiasm.

Your curiosity is a flicker of a flame. When you fuel it by paying attention to it, you have the best possible chance of discovering the things, the places, the people that will bring you maximum fulfillment. Why?

Your curiosity is directly connected to your internal motivation— the most powerful drive in your life.

All winners have internal motivation, a furnace fueled by love for what they do or what they achieve. It gives them the hunger and determination they need to win. You have one option for finding out what your best possible future could be: Follow your natural curiosity.

We all have unique interests. None of us can explain why we are attracted to certain things and have no use for others. Why does one person like sushi while another (me) hates it? Who knows? Some people love the law, some are led into medicine, some even say they love accounting. Who can explain any of it? The only thing we know for sure is that if we are going to lead rich, satisfying lives, we need to follow our instincts.

Our unique combination of interests is the key to our unique potential. When our internal furnace is burning, we stay engaged and energized. This is basic psychology. If you love sushi but are iffy on Greek food, you're going to be far more excited about going to a sushi restaurant than a Greek restaurant. Somebody who loves accounting is going to have a tough time being successful at something completely different.

You will never catch me on a high wire, but from his teenage years, Philippe Petit wanted only to be an aerialist. Then, at eighteen, he saw the sketches for the yet-to-be-built World Trade Center towers in a French newspaper while waiting to see a dentist. He grabbed a pencil, drew a line between the towers, and then spent six years studying, improving, and tackling bigger and bigger feats. After months of secret reconnaissance of the mostly completed towers, on August 7, 1974, he fulfilled his dream. Step by step, buffeted by the wind, he crossed from one tower to another along a thin cable. He did something no one had ever done, and nobody will ever do again.

Making the decision to go for what you want is a sales pitch you make to yourself. You're selling yourself on the idea that you can have more and do more. And you're selling yourself on the effort it will take to make it happen. Sales are emotional. Your heart has to be in it, or you won't be committed to giving it everything you've got. You have to push yourself to be successful. Unless you're doing something you really want to do, you won't have the drive. You'll take shortcuts, falter, and eventually give up.

On the flip side, when you turn on your internal motivation, it wakes you up to *all* the things you want to do, and you start finding ways to do them. And that makes life more exciting! You get out of the rut, out of the routine. You operate closer to your capacity. Why is that? Because you're doing what you want to do and tapping into your internal motivation—the most powerful motivation in the world.

UNTIL YOU FOLLOW YOUR WHIMS, YOU CAN'T KNOW WHAT YOU REALLY WANT

Every big idea starts out as a whim: "Hmm, wouldn't that be great?" Until we follow the idea, we can't be sure if we *actually* want it.

Let's say that I'm frustrated because I think I want to start a business, but I believe there is no chance for that to happen. So I don't pursue it. I don't do any research. I don't talk to business owners. I don't find a mentor. What's the point if I don't have a shot, right?

However, if I did do the legwork, guess what I might find: I don't really want to start a business after all. Now that I know what it's like, I know it's not for me. But because I've let myself be bullied into not trying, I stay frustrated, believing that I have a dream that is out of reach.

If instead I let myself believe it *is* possible, I do the research and find out faster that starting a business isn't as exciting as I thought it would be. That discovery frees me up to *move on to other things that are more interesting.* As I did my research into business ownership, maybe I discovered that I'm fascinated by developing new products or leading a team of people or serving others. Maybe I found out about a new up-and-coming company with a position that would be perfect for me. Regardless, I connect with what excites me. And now I have the drive to move forward and do something big.

"I've always wanted to be somebody, but I see now I should have been more specific."[3] This is a Lily Tomlin joke, but there's good advice behind it:

*Winners know that if you
don't figure out what you want,
you'll get whatever life hands you.*

The best way to figure it out is to believe that just about anything is possible if you put in the effort and pursue your whims until they lead you somewhere more interesting.

I started playing guitar in high school, and I really enjoyed it. For a while, I thought about trying to become a professional musician. I believed I had the dedication and drive to make it happen. I spent time around musicians, studied what their lives were like, how they found success. And I discovered a big problem: most musicians are on the road about 80 percent of their lives. Because I had traveled constantly as a kid, that was the worst thing I could imagine. So, being a professional musician wasn't for me. Instead, I kept playing the guitar as a hobby, and I still enjoy it. If I had let myself become frustrated by my "unfulfilled dreams of stardom," I might have given up on the guitar entirely and missed out on something that brings me a lot of joy.

Winners dig in on their ideas. They read about them, they talk about them, they connect with people, they ask questions. What are the possibilities? How do you go about it? They immerse themselves in the reality of it. The process gives them a chance to realize for themselves whether they want it or not.

Life is too short to pursue everything available to us, and that's where your natural curiosity becomes a tool for efficiency. It's like an internal Geiger counter that propels you toward the things that might provide the answers to your big questions. If you use it well, it can help you get organized and create the life you want faster.

It may take a while to get to the work you're most driven to do, but you can learn and accomplish a whole lot along the way just by taking advantage of the opportunities in front of you and pursuing what you're curious about right now. You'll discover the big thing you want to do next and you'll contribute your excitement and energy to the world.

Start with What You Know Right Now

In his book *How to Fail at Almost Everything and Still Win Big* (Portfolio, 2013), Scott Adams of *Dilbert* fame writes that in the beginning, he had absolutely no interest in becoming a cartoonist. He was, however, interested in being his own boss and making good money. He tried many businesses, but none of them took off. When the cartooning idea appeared, he followed his curiosity and checked it out. Eventually, what he discovered was his life's work. It became his passion.

Some of us are driven by a passion for a certain kind of work. For others it may be a passion for a particular industry, like the entertainment or music industry or professional sports or health care or police work. Others, like Scott Adams, are driven by the results the work provides—the lifestyle or the income. They want the freedom of running their own business or they want maximum income potential. And others want to make a contribution to their community or a cause.

I'm sure you have at least some idea about what you want your life to be—the level of success you hope for, the income you'll need, the hobbies you would like to pursue, the work you enjoy most. These are your starting points.

Just don't limit yourself when you're trying to discover how far to go with them.

PLAN, BUT DON'T OVERPLAN

—

*Do your due diligence, convince yourself that
what you want is possible, and then start.*

I have a friend, Joe, who was a very hard worker and always in a hurry to move forward. He told me once about an experience he had in one of his early jobs. He was twenty-three and working at a community loan company. He showed up early every day and closed more loans than anyone else at the branch. One day, as his manager came in, Joe said to him, "We need to talk."

"Sure," said the manager, happy to give his best employee some time. They walked into his office and sat down.

Joe started the conversation by asking, "How much do you make?"

Startled, the manager said, "I'm not telling you that!"

"Yes, you are. And I'll tell you why. I'm your best employee. I come in early. I stay late. I work hard. I close more loans than anybody else. I make you a lot of money. I do that because one day I want to move up and have a job like yours. But if I'm going to keep on doing that, I need to know what I'm working for."

Joe had made his point. So after a long pause, the manager said, "Fine!" He grabbed a piece of paper, wrote down a number and slid it across the desk.

Joe picked it up, read it, and then put it back on the desk. He was silent for a few moments. Then he stood up, said, "I quit," and walked out the door.

He couldn't get what he wanted where he was, so he moved on.

Joe was only twenty-three years old at the time, but he was a smart twenty-three-year-old—smart enough to look down the road to see where he was headed. He was going to work hard, and he wanted to make sure he got paid for it. When he found out that wasn't going to happen where he was, he moved on—immediately.

Before you work too hard on an idea or a possible goal, make sure it's worth it. Do your due diligence. Be skeptical. Ask every question you can think of. Test your assumptions. Double check what you've been told. Find out how much and how long it will take. Check out the competition. Be like Joe.

Make sure you know

- what it is you're working toward,

- if you have enough motivation and drive to achieve it,

- that you have the resources to pursue it,

- that it's something you'll enjoy doing, and

- what it will take to consistently make forward progress.

PLAN TO CONVINCE YOURSELF

Once you've decided that a destination is worth it, you need a road map to get you there. You need to get specific about how you are going to win, a framework for putting your skills and knowledge to work. As you move through any plan, you grow and your plan has to grow and change with you. But you need a general sense of the steps that will move you toward your goal. Otherwise you'll just meander along, wasting a lot of time and energy. As the old saying goes, failing to plan is planning to fail. Of course, you aren't supposed to worry yourself to death planning every possible detail. The idea is to have enough of a plan that you can see yourself making it work.

A plan also helps you stay on track once you get started. When you have broken down the big goal into smaller targets, you won't be as frustrated when things take longer or are harder than you thought they would be. Each time you hit a goal, you have a victory to celebrate. You'll be able to measure your progress, and that will give you a logical anchor to overcome the doubt that can creep in. When you're consistently moving forward, you don't get frustrated as easily and you don't stay frustrated for long. The next target is waiting for you, pulling you forward.

Most important, though, is this:

*Planning helps you convince yourself that this is something you **can** do and something you **should** do.*

It gives you the confidence to say, "The odds are strong that I can make this happen and the return will be worth the effort." The logical analysis helps you overcome doubt. When you already have the why (you really want it!) and you can see the how, you'll feel ready to jump in.

Pursue Reality, Not Fantasy

We live in the real world. We should all have hopes and dreams, but we have to make them happen in the real world. When we're planning, we have to balance our excitement about an idea with the probable returns on that idea and how capable we are of pursuing it right now.

I encourage you to chase your dream. But we all have to eat. So when you're planning, you have to ask yourself, Can I support myself by doing this?

Let's take career choice as an example. Some jobs are so competitive that only the elite get paid. There's a reason so many of the waiters in Hollywood consider themselves actors. There's a reason we all understand what the phrase "starving artist" means. Lots and lots of people want the "fun" jobs—actor, musician, artist. When it comes to the fun jobs, only the elite get paid. If you are going to pursue that type of life, you had better be sure that you have the drive—an obsession, really—to put in the hundreds of thousands of hours to make it. And that you don't mind sharing an apartment with six other people until you do.

If you don't have that kind of drive—the kind where you literally can't imagine doing anything else—be honest with yourself and find a way to make it a different kind of pursuit. Paul Allen plays the electric guitar and owns the Seattle Seahawks and the Portland Trail Blazers, among other companies. James Dolan, CEO of Cablevision, has a blues band. You can pursue passions without making them the foundation of your next career move.

Aside from the depth of your motivation, what if the plan you're developing presents other reasons that your goal or idea may not be possible? Again, ask yourself, how much do

I want it? If it's something you really want, you need to find a way to get into a better starting position. Ask:

- Am I just having trouble committing? Are there resources I could devote to this if I was fully committed? (Doing big things usually means sacrificing less important things. Are you willing?)

- Is the timing wrong? Do I have other obligations I need to deal with first? (If you have a young family you're trying to support, it might not be the time to go back to school or switch careers and take an entry-level job. You might need to build your financial security first.)

- Do I have enough experience to get started now? Or do I need to learn more, build certain skills, or connect with more people who could advise me?

If there are specific things holding you back or making it seem just too difficult, you can start doing smaller things to get into a better starting position. Do the advance work. Get mentally organized, deal with other obligations, save, learn, teach yourself if you need to. If you want it bad enough, you should be willing to do the early prep necessary to make it possible, even if you can't get to "go" right now.

Finally, in your planning, ask yourself, are the possible outcomes good enough—or do I want them enough—to make this worth my time? Make sure that even if it costs more, takes more time, requires more effort than you think it will, it's still going to be worth it to you. If it's not that important, don't even start. Remember what Jerry Seinfeld said: "Sometimes the road less traveled is less traveled for a reason."

DON'T GET STUCK IN THE PLANNING STAGE

There's planning and there's overplanning. Overplanning is just another form of doubt creeping in to kill your excitement and enthusiasm.

At some point we all say, "I want to jump to the other side of the fence." And we start by studying the fence. We consider what it will take to climb it. We peek through the pickets and examine the other side. We begin to plan how we'll get up and over. Which we should all do. We should think ahead. We should prepare for big changes. And sometimes the more we think about it, the less of a good idea it seems to be. We've avoided ending up somewhere we don't really want to be. But if we decide we want it, we eventually go for it and start climbing over.

But some people never hit that stage. They decide it would be best to take a course on learning how to climb fences. And then they spend a year studying different jumping techniques. And then they spend five years researching the details of the world on the other side. And they never get one foot up the fence. Because they are convinced they need The Perfect Plan. With the perfect plan, all the doubt will disappear.

I don't want to shock you, but no amount of planning is ever going to erase all doubt and no plan you can create is going to work perfectly. (Only God has that ability.) All the planning in the world doesn't counteract the fact that we cannot know the future. Even with a great plan, the unexpected occurs. Circumstances change. We hit obstacles. We have to backtrack. We continue to reevaluate, reassess, and adjust. (I'll talk more about adjustments in chapter 3.) Dwight Eisenhower said, "In preparing for battle, I have always found that plans are useless, but planning is indispensable." Planning helps you wrap your mind around what it will take and develop a general strategy for making it happen. But trying to turn a strategy into The Perfect Plan is a waste of time and energy.

When LPGA legend Annika Sorenstam was playing professionally she said she divided her time at the tee into two boxes: the think box and the play box. "What do you do in the think box? You think," she explained in a training tips video. "Should I have a 7-iron? Should I have an 8-iron? Is the wind in my face? Do I have an uphill lie?"[4] After you finish thinking, once you have a plan for the shot, you move to the next box—the play box. The think box is where you commit to your plan, the play box is where you execute it. If you don't move from the think box to the play box, you'll never make any progress.

The biggest danger of spending too much time in the think box of any project is that you might lose your initial enthusiasm for doing the thing. When it comes to most of our ideas, our enthusiasm has a shelf life. We won't be inspired to go for it forever. If you can't decide what you're going to do with your energy and drive, it will peter out. Doubt will grow and overwhelm you.

While losers are overdoing their thinking and planning, winners have moved on and are overdoing their activity and learning.

I'll get into this more in the next chapter, but for now, know that you should check out the big, obvious issues, but get your checking done before the idea goes stale. At some point you have to decide to jump the fence or you'll stay where you are for the rest of your life.

Plan enough to be convinced that it can work. Then jump in.

Every Choice Requires Adjustment

I worked with "Bullet Bob" Turley, Major League Baseball all-star and MVP, when I was just getting started in the insurance industry. He was one of the founders of the company, and I worked with him to build the business in Atlanta. We were trying to expand, we were trying to find new clients, and we were starting from scratch.

Every morning, for about three-and-a-half years, we would

meet in the office at 8:30 a.m. If he didn't have a new idea, I would. We would try that new idea for the day or for a few days until it ran out of gas. The next day we'd show up with a new idea. They all worked a little bit—we moved forward day by day. And we learned something.

The result wasn't exponential, mind-blowing growth in Atlanta. But when I went to North Carolina to open a new office and I was on my own, I had all of that experience behind me. It gave me an instinct and a feel for what would work and what wouldn't. I had a pantry full of methods for growing the business. It took a year to get the momentum going, and we only had 56 recruits to show for it. But once we had a base, all of that experience kicked in: in the second year, we had 1,800 recruits. In the third, we had 7,200 recruits. And in the fourth, we had 15,000 recruits. The first three years of constant experimenting and incremental improvements helped me develop a system to make the fundamentals work in our business. We could never have built that system if we hadn't tried a thousand different ideas, made a thousand different decisions to move forward, bit by bit. Along the way, we improved—something I'll dive into in chapter 5.

Every time you get ready to move down the field, you'll face decisions about what to do next. You'll have options, and you'll have to choose one. Even when we have the internal motivation we need, we can get stuck on those options. We're afraid we're going to make the wrong choice. But at some point, we have to turn decision into action. So what if it doesn't turn out the way you wanted? If that happens, you face the next decision and do something to get yourself back on track. Even if you've taken a detour, you've probably still made some progress and learned something along the way.

Winners take what they know right now and choose the best course of action they can.

Life doesn't always reveal itself all at once. What can seem impossible to understand today might make perfect sense tomorrow. Sometimes all you can see of the future is enough to take one more step. But that's all you need—at least right now. Take that step and then you'll see enough to decide on the next one. If it comes down to a this-way-or-that-way choice and there are no clear signs, go with your gut. What are your instincts telling you? In *My American Journey*, Colin Powell wrote, "I go with my gut feeling when I have acquired information somewhere in the range of 40 to 70 percent" (Ballantine, 2003).

At times, life is going to force you to choose from options that aren't super exciting. You simply might not be in a position to pursue what you want right now. When you face these moments, hesitating, delaying, or denying is not going to help you. It's going to work against you. You have to make the choice that seems to get you closer to what it is you want, even if only incrementally. Move forward in the right general direction and work hard to get access to better options soon.

I was talking to a friend of mine, Bill Whittle, in Baton Rouge about the dream home he and his wife, Leslie, were building. Building a home comes with hundreds of decisions. I asked him if the pressure of getting everything just right was getting to him. "No," he said. "Everything got easier once I realized that I couldn't lose. The new house will be a whole lot better than the one we're in now. If we get really dissatisfied with it at some point, we can always build another dream home." A good approach from another serial winner.

Usually, we don't have to make a lot of mistakes to get to the right answer. Usually, if your decision turns out to be the wrong one, you'll know pretty soon. Then you can jump onto another track. Every decision requires adjustments, even when we're dead sure we're making the right one. But you won't know what those adjustments are unless you choose and move forward.

YOUR CLOCK IS TICKING

If you want to win, the one decision you can't make is to *not* choose, to not do something. The only way you can lose is to not move forward.

If you feel like you're not making progress, ask yourself, What decision am I not making? Is it the big decision, the most important decision, to go for the life I really want? Or is it a more immediate decision that is keeping me from getting closer to that life?

At some point, you have to have enough belief in your destiny to take the next step. You have to go with what you have and start moving toward the future you want for yourself. Winners make the decision to go for the life they really want every single day, in small ways. Sometimes the decisions are easy, sometimes they're not. They do their best to lead a life without regrets—which doesn't mean a life without mistakes and losses, by the way.

It's not good enough to join the group who raise their hands and say they "want" more out of life. You have to join the group who are willing to put in the effort to make it happen. Making the decision to break out of the cocoon and do something big is the first step. And yes, you have to get emotional and excited about doing *something*—you need your internal furnace burning. But when it comes to running the race, you have to ask yourself, well, what am I going to do now?!

For now, I'll encourage you to start moving forward. Why rule yourself out? Why take other people's word for what's possible? Find out for yourself. Accept the truth that you are capable of achieving anything you want. Make the decision now to win. You're good enough to go for it.

It doesn't matter where you start. What matters is where you finish. The sooner you decide and start, the sooner you can get where you want to be.

THE
CYCLE
OF
WINNING

1 *DECIDE*

2 *OVERDO*

3 *ADJUST*

4 *FINISH*

5 *KEEP IMPROVING*

———————— |━━| ————————

CHAPTER 2

DON'T JUST DO IT,
OVERDO IT

Before its space shuttle fleet was retired in 2011, NASA ran more than 130 missions. With every single one, the stakes were astronomically high. The lives of the people on board, billions of dollars, the hopes of a nation, the future of the space program. So much was riding on getting these shuttles launched successfully and home safely.

For each of those missions, the most critical moments were the first eight minutes and thirty seconds after liftoff. Two solid rocket boosters would burn through 2 million pounds of solid propellant to generate 5.3 million pounds of thrust. The three main shuttle engines used 500,000 gallons of liquid propellant to generate another 1.2 million pounds. The goal was to reach a speed of almost 18,000 miles per hour. It took years of planning, months of training, and weeks of checks and rechecks to make this moment happen.

When the flight finally began—when somebody said, "We have liftoff"—what were the astronauts and the people in mission control doing? Well, we know they weren't sitting around drinking coffee with their fingers crossed. Every eye was on a monitor. Every finger was on a switch or button. They were making minor adjustments to throttle and pressure and oxygen levels. Everybody was working to make sure the shuttle broke gravity and got to orbiting altitude safely. Every second was critical. The solid rocket boosters would do their thing and then separate at about two minutes into the flight. The main engines would burn for another six-and-a-half minutes. The shuttle reached altitude and the astronauts maneuvered it into a safe position for the empty fuel tank to separate and fall back to Earth. And finally the shuttle and the astronauts were gliding safely in orbit.

That is the moment when everybody could *finally* breathe.

Were they possibly overdoing it? Absolutely not. The risk of failure at every moment was extraordinarily high. And those failures had actually occurred. Everyone at NASA was committed to making sure it never happened again. If I were an astronaut in training, I'd sure hope they were doing everything they could to get me up and down again safely.

Other than the lives at stake, consider this: all the fuel, the thrust, the speed, the focus, the attention, and the adjustments in the first ten minutes of a space flight make the next week or two in space possible and (almost always) successful.

We aren't all rocket scientists, but it isn't hard to see the value in a high level of early effort. In every new project or endeavor, winners follow the same principle. They overdo it in the beginning—with resources and effort—so that they can break the gravity holding them down. If they build up enough momentum, it will carry them through the friction they'll face on the way to their goal. The shuttle uses 2 million pounds of solid fuel and 500,000 gallons of liquid fuel to get into orbit. Guess how much it uses for the rest of a mission: less than 300,000 gallons. The momentum from liftoff and the gravitational pull of the Earth keeps it in orbit for days or even weeks. That's the kind of start winners know they need to make a successful trip to the top more likely.

Winners launch into every project with a mindset and plan to overdo it at the start. Because "just do it" isn't good enough.

The start makes or breaks everything that comes after. In the beginning, we never know exactly what it's going to take to win. We don't know what hurdles we're going to face. We have to create a competitive advantage by giving ourselves the best shot of succeeding early. And the only way to do that is to give it everything we have right from the start. Just going through the motions won't get it done. As it says in Ecclesiastes 9:10, "Whatever your hand finds to do, do it with all your might." Nobody has ever accomplished something great with a half-hearted effort.

Start with a bang, and you'll build the momentum and confidence to keep going when the going gets tough.

START WITH A BANG

—

Winners manage themselves to success by focusing on what they can control. Others get beat by letting their minds wander toward those things they can't control.

What's the number-one thing you can control to improve your odds of success? Your level of activity and effort.

If you wind yourself up to *just do it* you're setting yourself up for failure before you even begin. You will always face unknowns, disasters, and reversals. You need to allow for a margin of error. This is especially true the first time through. After you've done something a few times, you know more about it and your judgment and foresight improve. Of course, this is why winners look like wizards to all of those coming behind them. Newcomers don't know the price winners have paid for that knowledge and skill. And many people *never* learn this critical principle of winning:

It's doing the extras that add the extras to your life—that give you the biggest results.

When you overdo right from the beginning, you can quickly move through the basics that most people accomplish and on to the extras. If you get off to a slow, average start just doing the minimum, it will take forever just to master the basics. You may never make substantial progress. And that is the path to mediocrity.

Ask yourself again, do I want to do this or not? If you do, then jump in with both feet. Sticking your toe in the water isn't the move you need to build momentum. You can't be tentative.

Success is never guaranteed. Nobody knows the future. So all you can do is everything in your power to put yourself in position to win. Give it *everything you've got.* When you do, you'll overcome the tendency to underestimate. You'll develop the momentum you need to break through doubts, disappointments, and obstacles. And most important, you'll find success faster, build your confidence, and prove to yourself that you're capable of making it to the finish.

EVERYONE UNDERESTIMATES

Ask anyone who has ever built a house: no matter how hard you plan or how long you plan, there are always surprises. I was a construction supervisor for a real-estate development company for four years after I graduated from college. I oversaw the building of one hundred houses, and I can tell you that we had time and cost overruns on almost every one, no matter how hard we tried to avoid it. Why? Ninety-nine percent of the time, when something is built for the first time, it costs more than you budgeted. Sometimes a lot more. We were building a lot of homes, but rarely did we build the same home twice. It doesn't matter if you factor in a cushion. In home building, you spend 10 to 25 percent more than you expect to spend, 95 percent of the time. Why is this? Because life is complicated and full of surprises. No one knows the future.

If you want to get somebody in public works to laugh, ask them how many bridge or highway projects come in on budget. Actually, a University of Oxford business school professor did a study on this and found that 90 percent of the 258 big bridge, rail, road, and tunnel projects he looked at ended up over budget.[5] Millions over budget. Humans have been building this stuff for thousands of years. You would think we'd have gotten the hang of estimating by now.

But *no*. Everyone underestimates. Companies do it, governments certainly do it, and we do it. We set expectations for how much effort and resources we'll have to put into any new project or goal too low. We do it because we can't see into the future—and sometimes because we don't want to admit how hard a new endeavor might be. If we do, we might not go for it.

Underestimating is one of the biggest causes of failure. The

Why Winners Overdo

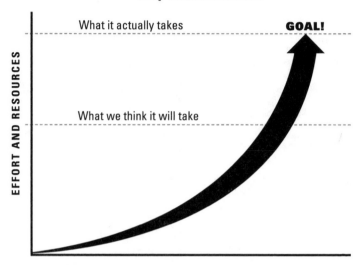

best way to combat it is by overdoing. Yes, we need a plan, but we have to start any project with the expectation that our plan is off by a good number of percentage points. We don't know how far off, so it's best to be safe.

The extra momentum we build by overdoing carries us across the first bumps in the road.

Early bumps are indicators that we'll need to put in even more effort and energy if we want to make it the rest of the way. If we don't have enough momentum early on, those bumps can be killers. When the going gets tougher than expected, many people assume the wrong thing: "Obviously, I'm not good enough. I can't do this." Don't fall for this idea. In fact, the early struggles we face with any project send a very simple message: Try again—and do more this time! Make an honest effort, one that gives you a real chance to succeed.

To avoid the biggest pitfalls of underestimating, give any new endeavor everything you can.

OVERCOMING BUYER'S REMORSE

Think about the last time you bought something big. You were so excited about it at the store or showroom. You paid the bill, brought it home, and within a few hours, you started noticing little things that just weren't quite right—or at least not what you expected. This doesn't look as good as it did in the store. Why are those buttons so far from the steering wheel? Is this tight around the shoulders?

We experience buyer's remorse in every new thing we start in life. I've never known somebody to start a new job and not have a hundred little doubts in the first week—about their new boss, about the work they thought they would be doing but aren't, about the company culture, about their commute. When we start something new, it's strange and uncomfortable. We are programmed to resist the unknown—it can be dangerous. So our doubt escalates and our energy starts to fail.

Dale Carnegie once wrote that the way to defeat fear and doubt is to "keep so busy and work so hard that you forget about being afraid."[6] We feel doubt so intensely the first week of a new job not only because we face so much newness but also because we often aren't very busy. When we don't have much to occupy our time, we start to dwell on the negatives— or possible negatives.

Want to get past the doubt you're likely to feel at the beginning of anything new? Fill your time with as much activity as possible. You'll kick out the doubt, reach your comfort zone faster, and have a better shot of maintaining your energy and excitement.

EARLY SUCCESS BREEDS CONFIDENCE

The statistics on usage of gym memberships are pretty sad. Only about 29 percent of people who sign up are actively using their membership after six months.[7] But studies have also shown that people who use the gym more than eight times in the first month tend to keep going.

You might have responded to that with, "Well, duh! Obviously people who go a lot in the first month keep going. They're the type of people who like it, so they keep doing it." Maybe. Or maybe it was just as hard for them as it was for anybody else. But by overdoing it at the beginning, when their enthusiasm was high, they saw some improvement— some success—faster. The results in the first month inspired them to keep going. Do you think that might have some-thing to do with it?

The best form of confidence is the confidence that comes from achievement.

This is why you overdo it at the start. Momentum deliv-ers massive mental and emotional gains. By making a strong effort early, while your initial enthusiasm is high, you get to your first successes faster and prove to yourself that what you thought and hoped was possible is *actually* possible. You can finish the project. You can make it happen. When you put yourself out there and get consistent positive feedback, you find the strength and courage to keep going.

Michael Jordan was known as a clutch shooter. In the final seconds of a game, if the team needed two points, the ball went to him. Where did this start? When he made the title-winning shot in an NCAA championship game as a freshman at the University of North Carolina at Chapel Hill. In an article for ESPN, he wrote, "The ability to perform in the clutch comes from having the confidence to know that you can. Where does that confidence come from? From having done it in the past. Of course, you have to do it that first time . . ." [8]

Early successes create a sense of confidence winners didn't

have when they started. As you get deeper into the project and you start running into unexpected challenges, you'll have a stronger backbone to stand up and face them. Every success under your belt makes you a little stronger, a little more confident, a little more prepared. Did Michael Jordan hit every last-second shot? Of course not! In fact in playoff games, he only made 50 percent of them (that's still amazing). But winners focus more on their wins than their losses.

A weak start often means you run into challenges before you've had a chance to create positive progress or results. You won't have the mental toughness to face them and keep on going. You're more likely to give up than you are to adjust and move forward.

Give yourself the best chance you can to be successful. Don't jeopardize your chances by holding back. Overdo it from the start and you'll build the momentum you need to make it to the finish.

THE FIVE KEYS TO OVERDOING

—

Nothing great happens with minimum effort. Plans are a good starting point, but it's the energy and effort you put behind them that make them fail or succeed.

People who feel like life is giving them a dirty hand usually resent everything they have to do. So they look for ways to cut corners. But if you only do the things you have to do—and even those not very well—you'll lead a small and limited life.

Serial winners don't mind laying it all on the line, driving themselves to exhaustion over a goal.

They know it's to their benefit. When you push yourself to overdo, you grow faster. You learn how to get more done. You learn how to make yourself more valuable. You pick up ideas and experience you can use the rest of your life.

So what's the strategy for overdoing? I've refined what I've learned from winners in all fields to five tactics, beginning with the Rule of Three.

THE RULE OF THREE

If you want to win, you have to play the odds, not let them frustrate you into giving up or playing small. You don't do just enough. You overdo in order to generate three times the opportunities you actually need. I've proven the Rule of Three about ten thousand times in my life.

The Rule of Three plays out in two ways. First:

> *Two out of the three times you try to accomplish something, it will go wrong.*

In baseball, somebody who gets a hit every third trip to the plate is batting .333, and that guy is an all-star! Only twenty-one players—including the greats like Ty Cobb, Ted Williams,

Joe Jackson, Lou Gehrig, and Babe Ruth—have had a career batting average higher than .333.

When our country was just getting started and the settlers in Virginia were beginning to cultivate corn, they would punch a hole in the ground and drop in three to six kernels, so they could guarantee at least two plants would grow. They had a lot at stake. If they didn't produce enough viable plants, they would have a very lean winter.

Does Starbucks or McDonald's have just one shop in any medium-sized town? Of course not. In the Gardens Mall in Palm Beach Gardens, Florida, there are two Starbucks. Both are in the middle of the mall but on opposite floors and opposite sides of the main corridor, diagonal from each other. These companies play the odds by having more than one location to maximize their returns in a geographic area. Now, they aren't counting on any of those locations failing, but they are counting on capturing traffic at each location that the other locations wouldn't.

Ohio State University did something historical as I was wrapping up the last draft of this book. They won the first College Football Playoff National Championship—and they did it with a third-string quarterback!

The second way the Rule of Three plays out is over time. If you have three possibilities or opportunities—three potential clients, three outlets for your product, three people on your team—they'll progress like the three hands on a clock.

One will move quickly, one will move slowly, and one won't seem to move at all but will eventually produce results. You had better have at least three rock-solid possibilities for every positive outcome you need in a certain time frame. Only one will deliver right away.

In my sales offices, we worked on commission. If we needed five teams to have strong production in a given month to hit our sales targets, I knew the only way I could keep my sanity was to maintain fifteen teams. That way, every month I'd have at least five good performers. They might be different every month, but I could count on five producing strong results.

When you're overdoing, think about how to give yourself the best shot at succeeding by making sure the odds are in your favor. Pay attention to Ecclesiastes 4:12: "A cord of three strands is not quickly broken." The Rule of Three isn't a rule to challenge. Instead, use it to strengthen your position and take your vulnerabilities out of play.

SET A BIG ACTIVITY GOAL

When I opened my own financial services office in North Carolina, as part of A.L. Williams & Associates (now Primerica), I had never been out on my own before. I had only worked as part of a team. And I was part of our company's expansion from Georgia and Florida into new geographical territory. It was daunting. I needed something to shoot for, to get excited about. The first critical step was to build a strong sales team. I didn't know how many recruiting appointments it would actually take, but I knew it would be a big number. So I set a goal: 500 appointments. "Even if it takes 500 appointments for me to get a core group in place, I'll do it." That's what I kept telling myself. It was a different kind of goal, because I knew I might not *need* to hit it. But it kept me focused on setting up as many appointments as possible every week. That was the road to success. You've heard it before: aim for the stars and you'll at least hit the moon. That's what I was doing.

In fact, it only took me 135 appointments before I had enough people on board to help me grow the business exponentially. It took three months, but I got those appointments done a lot faster than I would have if I hadn't had the big goal of 500.

You don't win by going for good. You win when you go for great. Winners use positive stress to their advantage. Positive stress comes from bigger challenges. Being courageous enough to tackle them gives you energy and excitement. It's a roller coaster—completely terrifying, but what a rush! Charles Schulz wrote, "Life is like a ten-speed bicycle. Most of us have gears we never use." Winners want to find those gears and discover just how fast they can go.

Unfortunately, we often set small goals, and small goals are killers. Small goals prevent us from connecting with our drive to excel. Small goals don't mean enough to inspire hard work. We simply can't get fired up about them, and we're beaten before we get started. When you are timid in setting goals I think your subconscious jumps to a conclusion: "Here we go again. He's not serious. He'll get distracted soon enough and forget all about it, so let's not focus on it. He doesn't really want to do it anyway."

On the other hand, when you decide to go for something big, something doable but a stretch, I think your subconscious says, "Whoa! We better get busy and come up with some ideas on how to pull this off, because I think he's really serious this time!"

Without a big goal, you don't really have a goal at all.

Winners set big activity goals daily, weekly, monthly—whatever makes the most sense. The goals are significant, but achievable. And because they are short term, each goal they achieve gives them the confidence they need to tackle the next goal tomorrow or next week or next month. And that's how they make fast progress.

Many people fail or quit, because they didn't give themselves lots of little targets to hit along the way. Without that consistent positive feedback to counteract the millions of tiny setbacks that can wear you down, they lose hope, confidence, and energy and give up. Five hundred appointments was a short-term goal that helped me get to a long-term goal of a hugely successful business. Marathon runners tackle challenging weekly mileage and time goals to improve their results at the next big race.

Find the courage to go for the big goal today! It will create excitement and anticipation. It will bring focus, clarity, and intensity to your efforts. And it will set the course for overdoing.

TRAIN TO FAILURE

My son, Adam, is a competitive bodybuilder. An approach to progress in his world is, "train to failure." What does this mean? In order to build muscle and strength, you have to lift a weight until you absolutely cannot do it one more time. There's a bit more to it, of course, but studies have shown that training to failure can increase human growth hormone and the size of muscle cells (which, of course, results in bigger muscles).

The same lesson applies to overdoing it. If you want to grow, you have to push yourself until you have nothing left to give. You can't grow your capacity if you don't use up all the capacity you have. You have to stretch the rubber band—it won't stretch itself and until it gets stretched it can't do you any good. You're the same way; we all are. If you never test yourself, you never improve. You overdo in the beginning especially, because that's when you have the most to learn and when you need to grow as fast as possible. You continue to push yourself throughout your life, because that is the path to serial winning. You use your capacity and strength, or you lose it.

> *Pushing yourself to uncomfortable limits today makes it possible for you to handle bigger challenges tomorrow.*

Primerica used to "volunteer" the top leaders in the field to come in to the corporate headquarters and provide insight. We were supposed to spend two days a week over ninety days showing the guys in the home office what was important to those of us in the field and what wasn't, what was helpful and what wasn't, and what needed to be improved. (Of course, they were nice enough to not give us a dime for our time.)

A friend and colleague, Andy Young, got "invited" and wasn't too happy about it. He was working all the time—in the office and on the road six days a week. How was he supposed to get his work done every week—for three months—in just three to four days? It was a nightmare for him in the beginning.

I saw him not long after his stint was over, and everything had changed. He now had two free days a week! He had had no choice but to figure out how to run his business in four days instead of six. It was possible after all. Andy wondered how much more time he was wasting, so he kept at it. He became so efficient and organized and established such strong priorities that he eventually found he could run his existing business in just two days a week. Now he had extra time to start some new expansion offices and experiment with new pilot programs, spend more time with his top performers, and also get in a bit of extra quality time with his family.

Andy would never have found all of that "free" time if he had not been put in a difficult situation to begin with. He had to push himself almost to the point of failure to learn, improve, and grow his capacity for doing. But in a short time he figured out how to adapt, and it changed his life. He had learned how to run his business rather than have his business run him.

Winners want to know what they're capable of. They are dying to find out just how hard they can push themselves. They live by the words of Airstream founder Wally Byam: "It was impossible, so it took a little longer to accomplish." And they know that pressure is their friend: it's what changes coal into diamonds. If you want to give yourself the best possible start, you need to put yourself in situations that seem impossible. Eventually, you'll grow through them.

Now, obviously, you can't do this all the time in every area of your life. Even bodybuilding experts say that if you just keep pushing to the point of failure, you'll hurt yourself. After every big push you need recovery time—a discovery that led to huge advances in training elite athletes. People who are focused on continual growth—as serial winners are—plan regular recovery time. It allows them to push for greater gains the next time.

Unfortunately—or maybe fortunately for you—most people won't push themselves hard enough to even need that recovery time. They spend much of their life worrying about "balance." For winners, balance isn't an all-the-time priority. What's important is taking advantage of opportunities when they are available. If it's harvest time and there's rain coming, everyone on the farm may go a few days missing meals and sleep to get the crop in. Family life gets thrown out of balance. So what? They know as soon as harvest is done they can get back to meals together and other priorities. At that point, balance isn't the big priority. The priority is getting the job done.

Here's the bottom line: By training to failure in the beginning, you'll set yourself on the path to build the strength and endurance you'll need long-term.

THE MacGYVER PRINCIPLE

Bill Orender, one of the greats in the financial services business, once told me how he starts his day: "I get up every morning, go to the refrigerator, pour myself a glass of orange juice, and remind myself that the cavalry is not riding to my rescue today."

Life is not going to hand you three or four or five times the energy and talent and resources you actually need to get things done. To get started you've got to go with what you've got and worry about reinforcements later. What does that mean? If you want to do big things, you'll need to leverage every resource available to you to progress as far as possible. It's only when you get to the farthest limit of your resources that new resources appear. This is called growth.

Winners "MacGyver" their way to the top. They are as creative, clever, and industrious as they can be in getting the most out of what they have. They understand a fundamental truth about life:

> ### *It's not what you have that matters, it's what you do with what you have.*

At each stage in the plan, they go as far as they can with what they have and what they know. While winners are turning a rubber band, dental floss, and some borax into a lasso to swing toward the next goal, losers sit around whining about everything they need and don't have. Winners know that the little things matter, and can lead to greatness. Luke 16:10 states it well: "One who is faithful in a very little is also faithful in much."

This is the biggest difference between people who *never* get things done and people who are *always* getting things done.

Those in the "never do" group are always preoccupied with all the things they don't have and believe they need before they can get started. The "get-'er-done" group goes on the attack, using whatever is available.

We all have tools and resources that we can leverage to develop an advantage. Some are obvious—experience, skills, talent, knowledge, even money. In particular, winners maximize their strengths. They know that doing great things usually means doing more of what you're good at and less of what you're lousy at. So they find ways to minimize their weaknesses in their approach. The more they exercise their strengths, the more obvious those strengths become. Soon, people stop asking them to do the things they're lousy at.

> *The truth about winning is that you have to start where you are and with what you have **right now**.*

You don't really have a choice—you can't deny reality. The good news is that where you are and what you have are enough to get you where you want to be.

DO THE THINGS OTHERS
AREN'T WILLING TO DO

A friend of mine wanted to learn to paint. He met a master painter and asked if he would consider tutoring him. The master said, "Yes. But first, go paint one hundred paintings. Until you do that, our time would be wasted."

Everyone wants the glory, no one wants to do the grunt work. Winners make themselves do it anyway. Why?

Grunt work leads to greatness.

Greatness is possible for almost everyone, but it requires doing the grunt work most would rather avoid. Amelia Earhart said, "Never do things others can do and will do if there are things others cannot do or will not do." Grunt work doesn't scare winners. But living a small, boring life does.

Winners take a unique position on grunt work to keep their attitude and energy up: Do what you *have* to do so that you can do what you *want* to do. Even if you love your business, career, job, or goal, there will always be tedious things that have to be done to win. Those are the things that the average and mediocre can't get themselves to do. It's the "doing what you don't want to do" that puts you ahead of the pack, especially at the beginning. The good news—and the bad—is that most of the grunt work comes early on the path to any big goal.

Success has two rules:
1. Pay full price. 2. Pay in advance.

Paying the conditioning price is where you can leave your competition behind. Your most valuable education will come from what you teach yourself while pursuing what you love. As a result, you earn a little more experience, skill, and toughness than those who took the easier path. It might not even show— that is, until the pressure is on and it's winning time.

Winners don't spend all their time doing grunt work, obviously. Once they've learned what they need to know, they find a way to turn that grunt work over to somebody else. Or to innovate and minimize it. It becomes a game: How efficient can they be? How fast can they get it done? It's the Andy Young approach. While a winner is working smarter *and* harder, others are trying to get there either with less effort or without taking the time to learn and improve.

Yet winners also know that every new challenge, every new big goal comes with a new set of grunt work. Even the extremely successful spend time every day on grunt work. Because they are always at the beginning of something. And they know they have to overdo it if they want to succeed.

THE LAW OF AVERAGES AND THE LAW OF HIGH NUMBERS

—

When you're doing big things, you can't measure what it will take long-term to win based on what it takes in the beginning. You've got to break gravity.

At the beginning of the chapter, I told you the story of the space shuttle launches. Do you think the people in mission control are ever sitting there saying, "Wait a minute . . . how many miles per gallon does this baby get?" They don't measure miles per gallon because the thing that matters most is getting the first 200 miles into the sky. The fuel they use to travel the *17,500 miles per hour* for the rest of the week barely matters!

You've got to overcome inertia. It takes an incredible expenditure of energy to start. Once you get into orbit, everything changes. The momentum from overdoing it early on keeps you going, so you can pull back on the throttle. Now, you can't win by simply coasting (this is a trap that even winners can fall into after they've had some success). But the start is always the hardest part of winning.

Think about how hard it is to get yourself to start going to the gym. You have to pick a gym, sign up, give them a big check, ask yourself if it's worth it, buy some new sneakers, go the first time, stay with it the first week, get through those awkward feelings of not know what to do, get a pattern going . . . You have to expend a lot of energy before it starts to feel natural! And that's why so few people keep at it. Remember the statistic I shared early in the chapter? Only about 29 percent of people are actively using their membership after six months.

Consider how hard it is to launch a new project. Planning, building the team, figuring out how the team will communicate, acquiring the necessary resources, trying early ideas, regrouping when those ideas don't work out, getting everybody ahead on the learning curve. There's a reason we have an entire profession—project management, which even has a certifying body—devoted to this work. There's a phrase in business: the project graveyard. It captures the hundreds or thousands of projects that die an early death in companies every year. The number-one reason they fail? The same reason most new businesses fail: not enough effort or resources were devoted to making them successful. They tried to do it with the bare minimum, or maybe a bit more than that, when they should have been overdoing it. And when they didn't make good progress, they abandoned it altogether.

Every new project or endeavor is challenging in the beginning, and so most people (and teams) quit before they really get started. They say to themselves, "Well, if this is what it's going to take, I'll never be able to win. If I have to work this hard for just a little bit of results, I'll never make real progress. I quit." They're like turtles. They poke their heads out of their cocoons, get frightened by what they see, and withdraw into the security of what they've always "known."

Unfortunately, their thinking is wrong. They make the first expenditure of effort and immediately start applying the law of averages, which is too soon.

Winners accept that the law of averages only kicks in once you've activated the law of high numbers.

Doing something for a week or a month or sometimes even a year doesn't give you a big enough sample size to calculate valid averages. That makes as much sense as asking five people on the street what their favorite ice cream is and then assuming you know the most popular flavor in America. (It's vanilla; but chocolate is the most popular milkshake flavor.) Or watching a baseball player strike out in a game and assuming his career batting average is .000. To be accurate, you need to know how he performed every time he was at bat.

The only way to calculate an average that is meaningful is to apply the law of high numbers. In Las Vegas, the casinos calculate payout percentages based on hundreds of thousands of people playing the games. Insurance actuaries base their cost assessments for car insurance or life insurance on actuarial tables—which are based on data from millions of insurance holders. The law of averages *plus* the law of high numbers improves estimates and forecasts.

In the beginning of anything new, you don't have the data. So don't base a potentially life-altering decision on a tiny bit of information. Focus on a ton of activity and worry about the law of averages later.

EARLY STRESS HELPS YOU SUCCEED

The stress you feel early on is no different from the effort you have to expend. It's greater in the beginning. Starting something new is always high pressure. You're not sure exactly how you are going to win, or if you can even pull it off. But that stress keeps you on your toes. The pressure keeps you moving, keeps you sharp. It keeps you from getting lazy and complacent. All learning and growth is stressful. Only the coffin offers a stress-free existence.

That said, remember when you learned to drive, arrived for

your first day on the job, or went on your very first date? Do these things stress you out now? No, of course not. And why is that? Because you have practiced them enough to become comfortable in your own abilities. You have mastered the skill. Simple as that. Over time, the pressure of anything new will reduce—and you'll be ready to put yourself into a different high-pressure situation!

This is why winners overdo it at the start. They know that while you can't guarantee success, you can put the odds in your favor—substantially—through lots of activity as fast as possible. They activate the law of high numbers first so that the law of averages kicks in and success becomes a statistical event. If you're doing enough of the right kind of activity, eventually, you will see some success. And eventually you will learn how to become more effective and efficient. That's what allows you to pull back on the throttle.

For now, take a deep breath and say the following: It will not always take this much effort. It will not always be this confusing. It will not always feel so awkward. It will not always be this stressful.

Stick with it. You *will* get better. And eventually, like the rocket, you'll hit your orbit.

* * *

If I've learned anything about winning, it's this: You can't piddle your way to greatness. You have to give it everything you've got. If you want to win, don't waste time giving it a halfhearted effort. Focus on getting past start as fast as you can. Build momentum. When you get it, leverage it for as long as you can. As soon as you start to slow down, increase your activity to get it back.

When obstacles pop up, you'll have the speed and force you need to adjust quickly and blow past them.

THE
CYCLE
OF
WINNING

1 DECIDE

2 OVERDO

3 ADJUST

4 FINISH

5 KEEP IMPROVING

CHAPTER 3

DON'T QUIT, ADJUST

When I was a sophomore in high school, we lived at Camp Darby, a US military base near Livorno, Italy, right on the Mediterranean. At the time, there were two other US bases with high schools in Italy, one in Vicenza and one in Naples. We actually had a football season: we played eight-man football and the season was four games long.

Our high school had about one hundred students, Vicenza had a couple hundred, and Naples had about eight hundred students. Obviously, there was no league balancing based on school size. If we wanted to play football, we had to play Naples.

One Friday night, we were hanging out at the base cafeteria. The next day we had a game against Naples, and they were staying on the base, hanging out in the cafeteria too. It was really the only place to go. Of course, we knew that we faced impending doom. We were going to get slaughtered the way we were always slaughtered by Naples. The vibe in the room was tense.

I was sitting at a table when a guy from the other team walked by, handed me a card, and kept on walking. Here's what the card said:

> Your story has touched my heart.
> Never before have I met anyone
> with as many problems as you.

The words on that card have stuck with me over the years. In fact, I made my own version and keep a big stack close at hand. First, it makes me laugh every time I read it. Second, it presents a simple truth: Just like our competitors, life will show us no sympathy. We are not owed any special favors. Sooner or later, we all find ourselves in tough spots, with circumstances lined up against us. The easy thing to do is rant about how life has dealt us a bad hand. It's not *fair*.

Whining won't change anything. We all face challenges. The more important your goal, the more likely it is that you'll run into problems along the way. You might as well stand up, take what comes, and do the best you can. The only other option is to quit. But that is the option of misery, of unfulfilled dreams.

Yes, we went out on the field the next day and they slaughtered us, just like we all knew they would. But here's the rest of the story.

We also played basketball, and because there was so little to do on the base or in the town, we played against the GIs at the base gym all year round. We got pretty good. But our coach was a formula guy and made us run plays. He wouldn't let us just play, and we were never able to really show what we were capable of on the court. But when basketball season rolled around and it was time to play Naples, we said, "Forget Coach. Let's just beat these guys." We went out on the court and went berserk. And we slaughtered them. I've forgotten all the other games, but I remember that one. It felt very, very good.

No one wins them all. But here's the good news:

You don't get just one second chance. You get chance after chance to achieve what you really want. As long as you don't fall down, roll over, and quit.

When serial winners face challenges, pitfalls, tragedies, and disasters, they pick themselves up, adjust to the new reality, and keep going. They *don't quit*. Because they know that defeat isn't permanent until you do.

WIN ANYWAY

—

*When we're down and looking up at those who
have reached the top, it can seem like they've never
faced any big challenges.*

They haven't faced the same problems that threaten to crush your hopes and dreams. They have no idea what it's like to suffer. They have no baggage to hold them back. They've never been fired, dealt with bad credit, gone bankrupt, applied for unemployment, lived off food stamps, or been homeless. They've never faced family problems, health problems. They've never doubted, felt overwhelmed, considered tossing in the towel. In fact, they are rarely bothered by the cares and interruptions of life that most of us face. They've lived problem-free and the result is pure success.

Ridiculous!

How Progress Really Happens

No one leads a completely protected life. Just as we under-estimate the effort and resources it will take to win, we expect the path to our goals to be smooth. Of course, it never is. Regardless of who you are or where you come from, you will face trials and tribulations as long as you live on this earth. Look closely and you'll discover that the successful, the champions, the heroes have all collected scars: physical, mental, emotional, and psychological.

Terry McGhee, a New York Police Department detective who joined the antiterrorism task force after 9/11, is one of the primary investigators responsible for apprehending Sulaiman Abu Ghaith, Osama bin Laden's son-in-law. Now, Bin Laden had about twenty-five kids (that's what you can accomplish with five wives) and lots of sons-in-law, but Abu Ghaith, the chief spokesman for Al Qaeda, was responsible for spreading its influence with the younger generations of Islamists and was allegedly one of the founders of an organization in America that was raising money for Al Qaeda prior to 9/11. You can imagine how focused Terry McGhee was on finding this man and bringing him to justice.

But in 2008, Terry broke his spine in a surfing accident in Lisbon, Portugal, where he was gathering intel. What did he do? Give up? Retire? No. He did everything in his power to get back to the investigation. Just a few months later, bound to a wheelchair, unable to move his fingers, he was hunting for the members of Al Qaeda again. He leveraged all the knowledge he had gained over the years and continued to review video footage and witness statements and coordinate with overseas counterparts. In 2013, Abu Ghaith was finally captured. If Terry McGhee hadn't been on the case, there is a good chance this never would have happened.

Everybody has scars. Life goes on. And so do winners.

Winners know they're going to face hurdles, obstacles, failures, tragedies, and disasters—the same as everybody else.

Ecclesiastes 9:11 says "The race is not to the swift or the battle to the strong, nor does food come to the wise or wealth to the brilliant or favor to the learned; but time and chance happen to them all." No one is exempt from problems or injustice.

So how do serial winners do it? By getting there anyway. They make a stupid mistake—they win anyway. They lose out on a great opportunity—they win anyway. They face a devastating disaster—they win anyway. They don't focus on what has gone wrong—they focus on how to win anyway. They refuse to be defined by the negative things that happen in their lives.

WINNING MEANS OVERCOMING

Clint Eastwood delivered one of my favorite lines in one of my favorite movies, *Heartbreak Ridge*: "You improvise, you adapt, you overcome." He was talking to US Marines, but it's true of any winner facing an obstacle. Serial winners in particular are overcomers. We often can't imagine the many ways in which they have had to improvise, adapt, and overcome. The painful "grinding" on the way to the top is obscured by the glamour and glory that comes after they got there.

John Lennon (not the Beatle) is a colleague of mine. When he first started working with me, over thirty years ago, he was in a tough spot. He was a successful entrepreneur and had decided to invest in a commercial real-estate develop-ment project with a partner. Unfortunately, the investment went south, the partner skipped town, and John was left with $400,000 in debt.

I didn't learn about this story until John and I had been working together for more than twenty years. When I first began to work with him, I saw him as a smart, driven, entrepreneurial guy who was focused on winning, and winning as quickly as possible. He not only didn't moan or complain about his tough situation, he never even mentioned it! He just got to work finding a way to resolve it.

Today, John is the leader of a company that spans fifteen states. He helped develop the Center for Entrepreneurship and E-Business at North Carolina A&T State University by establishing an endowed professorship. He is known nationally for his philanthropy. If he had fallen down and given up when he was facing the repercussions of a lousy deal and an unethical partner, none of that would have happened.

When you're knocked down, the choices are simple: give in or get back up and move forward. Problems can crush you or provoke you. It's a battle and the outcome depends on your response. If you give in, you lose. If you fight back, you can break through and keep moving forward. That's the only way to stay in control of your life. The only other choice is to give up and give in. If you do that you lose your dignity, your freedom, your independence. You become a victim. Don't do that.

People who have lived easy lives often lack the stomach for conflict. When I was growing up and playing sports, we called them "pretty boys." They never developed a competitive spirit and it ruined them. They weren't accustomed to fighting for what they wanted, and that made it hard for them to improve enough to get it. You can achieve great things if you're willing to compete for them. Life says, "You say you want this? Prove how much. Fight for it, earn it."

See, the drive to overcome and the drive to improve are intertwined—you can't do the first without doing the second. Actor Mark Ruffalo went through eight hundred auditions— eight hundred rejections!—before he got his first real acting job. Since his inauspicious beginnings, he's been in dozens of movies and he's been nominated for an Academy Award. Don't you think that with each audition, he got a bit better? Winners know that every failure contains a lesson they can use to improve their chances in the future. And if they keep improving, stacking the odds in their favor, eventually they'll win—and win more. As Winston Churchill once said, "Kites rise highest against the wind, not with it." When you choose to face your circumstances head on, you do greater things.

You don't have a shot of winning if you can't overcome the hurdles that you'll face.

QUITTING IS (USUALLY) STUPID

My mother and I were driving home from services at the First Baptist Church in Enid, Oklahoma. I was eight years old, and my dad was stationed at Vance Air Force Base. She and I were alone in the car, and I remember the conversation like it was yesterday.

You often hear successful people say, "My mother/grandma/dad always said . . ." and then they run off some nifty saying about getting ahead in life. That wasn't my family. My parents were concerned about the basics—eat, sleep, school, homework, church, stay on schedule, be good. No pithy philosophies for success. Except this time.

For some reason, the subject of quitting came up, and Mom said forcefully, "Never quit!" And then she shared this analogy: Our will for what we want in life is like a wooden block. When we quit, we roll it over. Each time you roll it over, the edges become dulled a little. And that makes it easier to quit the next time. Before long your will becomes soft around the edges, and you don't have the strength to stick with anything. "So don't quit!" she told me. "Don't get started."

I don't know why I remembered that little conversation, but I did. The lesson became a part of who I am. As I grew older, like everyone, I had some tough challenges. But I never quit. And I believe that fact has saved me from a lot of misery.

The Advantage of Compounding Effort

You're driving from New York to LA and you are finally thirty miles outside of the city. Suddenly the traffic slows and you see a sign that says, "Road closed due to mudslide." Do you turn around and drive home?

You save up your whole life to fulfill your dream of owning a Ferrari. You buy it, drive it around—very carefully—for a week. One morning, the engine won't turn over. Do you return it to the dealer?

Why quit something you've invested a lot of time and energy into accomplishing? Why not just dig down deep, figure out a solution, and keep going?

I have watched so many people work so hard for a goal, putting in tremendous amounts of blood, sweat, and tears. And then, for one reason or another, they get overwhelmed and quit. The big disaster is that their personal investment is washed away and they never receive the benefit of all their hard work. "Effort only fully releases its reward after a person refuses to quit," wrote Napoleon Hill.

People who have a pattern of quitting never get ahead in life—they never stay with anything long enough for their efforts to compound.

Thinking about quitting is not the same as quitting. Everybody has times when they think about it. It's normal. I have certainly thought about quitting in my career. For instance, I had been in the insurance industry for a couple of years when I was offered an opportunity to become a construction superin-tendent. It had been a tough two years. We were living hand to mouth, and the stress was breaking me down. The new oppor-tunity offered a regular income and a chance for us to gain a little traction financially.

I wasn't sure what to do. I was on the edge. So I called Art Williams, the president of our company. I tried to be clever. "Art, I have a guy on my team [I might as well have said 'friend' and put it in air quotes] who's been here for a couple of years. He's thinking about making a move, that maybe it would be smart to take a time-out, regroup, get organized, catch up financially, and then come back with a vengeance down the road." I didn't use the word *quit*.

Art saw right through it. "Larry, I think you would be mak-ing the biggest mistake of your life. You've got two years of priceless experience behind you. You're just on the verge of making it pay off. Why would you throw that all away now, when you've already done so much of the hard work?"

What he said certainly took some of the appeal out of quit-ting. I *had* worked hard, and I didn't want that effort to be a waste. So I settled down and focused. I made the next logi-cal move, and then the next one, and then the next one. Two years later, my income had doubled. Four years later, it had increased tenfold.

Quitting can quickly become a bad habit, it's true. And that can ruin your life. But what makes it a stupid move is that most people quit when success is right around the corner. If they had made it past one last hurdle, or maybe two or three, they would have won. Now, I had a few more hurdles in front of me when I had my chat with Art, and I had more moments of doubt. But my mother's advice and his stuck with me and I made it through.

Quitting sometimes seems like a great option—until you do it. After an initial (and false) sense of relief, you'll be just as miserable as you were before you quit. You've abandoned what you really want, you still have the same problems, *and you've given up your best option for solving them.* You're forced to choose from the least of bad options, and that is the path to misery.

High achievers think about quitting all the time. Anytime you're doing something great, challenging, and complex you operate in a pressure-packed environment. When you're trying to do big things fast, the stress can be overwhelming. I've heard many say they think about quitting two or three times every day. If you don't feel the same way you're probably not involved in anything very special or exciting. Of course, high achievers don't quit. The thought just pops into their head from time to time. They consider it for a second or two. And then they get back to work, making the next adjustment, leveraging all the effort they've put in so far.

Cheating: The Long, Slow Road to Quitting

At some point on the trip to the top, everyone faces one particular temptation: cheating. And the temptation usually crops up when we're facing an obstacle that we can't see our way around. Cheating is a form of quitting. You're quitting your effort to build lasting success and a positive reputation and legacy. The day you decide to cheat is the day you quit and the day you lose, even if the results don't appear for weeks, months, or years.

Cheating is a loser's game. Sooner or later it will always backfire and humiliate you.

But wait! Winners cheat all the time, don't they? Isn't that what people say? They only win because they lie, trick, con, and deceive. They cut corners, take credit for others' work, and make backroom deals. They don't care how many bodies they leave behind in their march to the top. They lack conscience. They ignore ethics and principles. They say and do whatever it takes to get ahead. In today's dog-eat-dog world, their approach seems to be the only way to really make it. The old adage remains as true as ever: Nice guys finish last.

This is the kind of BS cheaters use to justify their behavior. And to be fair, they are shown proof by the media almost daily that it's true. Lance Armstrong, Enron executives, most of the governors of Illinois for the past three decades, baseball heroes, Martha Stewart, Bernie Madoff—the list of people who cheated their way to winning seems never ending. But it seems that way only because cheating winners get 90 percent of the airtime and ethical winners get the rest.

Instead of focusing on what the famous cheaters do and how you might need to do the same to get ahead, focus on this: *All of these people got caught eventually.* Cheaters always do, one way or another. In the beginning they say to themselves, "Who will know? No one will ever find out." But someone always does. As the old adage goes, the wheels of justice grind slowly, but they grind exceedingly fine. If you're short-cutting the system, if you're lying or deceiving people just to get ahead, sooner or later your house of cards comes tumbling down. And when it happens, the consequences are devastating. All gains are lost, wiped out. What remains is a terrible and permanent stain.

Bernie Madoff's two sons shouldered much of the weight of their father's Ponzi scheme. They both worked at his securities business, and they were the ones responsible for his investigation by the FBI—they turned him in when they realized the company financials were "off." One son blamed his cancer relapse on the stress of the investigation and the other hanged himself on the two-year anniversary of his father's arrest.

When you face an obstacle, don't be tempted to take the easy way out. The key to your character can always be found in how you choose to face adversity. Your choices, good and bad, play an integral part in the story of your life. Ask yourself, How do I want my story to read? How will I be remembered by my children, grandchildren, friends, and neighbors? Do I want one-time, short-time, or all-the-time success?

Who wants to reach the top while trying to hide stinking piles of dirty laundry? On the outside you have all the trimmings of success, but it must be miserable to live with all that guilt and worry eating away at you. The emotional and mental toll of cheating is much more costly than just doing it the right way. People with character know it's not worth it. You need a clear conscience to have a clear mind—so you can focus on solving the next problem, taking the next step, or pursuing the next opportunity.

The most powerful stories about the value of not cheating are never told. It's the politician who chose not to take a bribe. It's the construction company exec who chose to spend the money on the right materials rather than the cheap (and possibly unsafe) alternatives. Sometimes people talk about those moments, but often they don't. Instead we hear all the bad stories.

Despite those stories, it's so easy to get sucked in. And then you're hooked. You can't get out. One lie or cheat leads to another leads to another. That's what thirty-five Atlanta Public Schools educators and administrators found out in March 2013, when they were indicted on charges of racketeering and corruption. The investigation found that almost 180 people were involved at forty-four schools. What were they accused of? Changing answers on standardized tests to improve scores—and to get bonuses or at least protect their jobs by "creating" such improvement! Once the cheating started, they couldn't stop, because test scores would drop. It went on for more than a decade. In the end, dozens lost their jobs and careers, and some are facing serious criminal charges.

People who cheat want to avoid the struggle, the cost, or the fight. They don't know the truth about winning:

Nothing of value in this world comes easy. The only way to get anywhere worthwhile is to go to work.

You don't need to cheat to win. It's a myth. In fact, you're almost ensuring that you won't win in the long term. As it says in 2 Timothy 2:5, "The athlete is not crowned unless he competes according to the rules." True winners don't cut corners to achieve short-term success or to get around an obstacle. You can't discover the cure for cancer by faking it and you don't unravel the genetic code by cheating. If you want results, your only option is to crank up the effort and face what comes.

Only a shortsighted fool is willing to risk his career, reputation, and legacy for a little short-term advantage. Achievement to be enjoyed has to be earned.

THE DIFFERENCE BETWEEN
ADJUSTING AND QUITTING

Sometimes the only adjustment that makes sense is to change plays entirely. If you've run a play to the best of your abilities and it's not moving you forward, it's time to call a new play. As W.C. Fields said, "If at first you don't succeed, try, try again. Then quit. No use being a damn fool about it."

When is quitting not quitting? When it's changing direction. When you realize the road you chose is not taking you to exactly where you thought it would, you change directions. When you get into a project and discover it isn't productive, fun, or fulfilling, you change directions.

*Serial winners don't quit. They **will** adjust goals and start racing in a new and better direction when it is the smart move.*

Quitting is giving up. Quitting is moaning, "Why bother? Why try? I'm just not good enough. It's just too hard." Changing directions is making a confident decision to go for what you want. If you don't make that move, your energy and excitement will dribble away and you won't be able to make it past the hurdles that come.

Finding the right career path, in particular, is like a dog settling down to sleep. He doesn't just lie down. He keeps moving around until he's comfortable. Only he knows when he's found the exact right spot.

When they first developed the certified financial planner certification (CFP) for people in the financial services industry, I thought, "I need that. My competitors are going to have it and I'll lose business if I don't." So a colleague and I signed up for the required twenty-five-week course. I completed the first of the five required sections and when the moment came to order books for the next section I said, "You know what? I quit." Here's why: I had learned that the CFP certification was designed for people who wanted to sell more and more complicated financial products to people with lots and lots of money. That's a very small percentage of the market and it wasn't what *I* wanted to do. Why waste twenty more weeks of my time? I didn't quit because it was too hard (I aced the test at the end of the first section) or too time-consuming. I quit because to me, it was meaningless. But I had no way of knowing that until I investigated it.

Every day, people quit their jobs. People quit bad habits. People quit bad relationships. People quit towns or cities. Because sometimes quitting is the best first step to adjusting your direction toward the life you really want. That's not quitting, that's changing directions. That's upgrading.

Trust your instincts—only you know the right choice,

based on what you want. If you've got a glimmer of a shot and you really want it, work against all odds. On the other hand, keep your eyes open. Make sure you're grounded in reality. Are you *really* a spectacular singer? Do you *really* have an affinity for languages? Can you *really* start training for the Olympics at this point in your life? It's great to want to prove people wrong, but if *you're* wrong, admit it and move on. Don't let yourself be delusional. As the Dakota wisdom goes, when you discover you're riding a dead horse, the best strategy is to dismount. The challenge is recognizing that the horse has died.

If you seem to be running into problems that just can't be solved—brick wall after brick wall after brick wall—ask yourself, is my timing off? Sometimes, the timing for a new project or endeavor just isn't right. You've gone as far as you can go right now and you need to let things resolve themselves a bit before you can go any further. You need to wait for a more receptive environment, more resources to work with, a stronger economy, or some changes in your personal life that might free up some energy or time. Be prepared to ask this question and accept the answers you find. Then adjust directions temporarily, but keep making general forward progress.

The worst thing is to stall out. Don't wait too long to switch plays. Don't waste time doubting, overthinking, or overplanning. Most of the people I've met who have made a big adjustment have said, "I wish I'd done it years ago. I don't know what I was waiting for." Remember, the clock is ticking so keep moving forward, one way or the other.

*   *   *

If you are pushing toward something that you really want, don't give up, don't give in. Don't quit! It will be the worst decision of your life. How do you get back up when you feel it's futile to continue? Give yourself a reality check and reconnect with your internal motivation.

USE FACTS FOR GUIDANCE
AND EMOTION FOR FUEL

—

*We all get depressed when things don't work out as
we had hoped, but winners don't stay depressed.*

You may be tired of hearing about the amazing Michael Phelps, the most decorated Olympic swimmer of all time. I'm not going to bore you with more stories of his awesome achievements. You can read his Wikipedia page. However, one event from the 2012 London Olympics is worth a closer look.

Going into the London Olympics, Phelps was the hero *and* the man to beat. Everyone was gunning for him—even Ryan Lochte, his teammate and the person who might have been the proud owner of the medals Michael had won in previous competitions. The first finals race for Phelps was the 400-meter individual medley. Millions of viewers were watching.

The stands were packed. Everybody was waiting to cheer for him at the finish.

And then Phelps came in *fourth*. Lochte took the gold.

Obviously, this was a huge blow for Phelps. And if he had let it bring him down or keep him down, it would have ruined his chances for the rest of the Games. But we know that didn't happen. Instead, Michael went on to win four gold medals and two silver medals, cementing his spot in the record books. So how did he do it? How did he stay on track and bounce back so quickly? Two ways:

- He accepted the facts and used them to guide him.

- He controlled his emotions and used them as fuel.

We know this by what he said in interviews and online.

First, Phelps accepted the blame. "It was just a crappy race,"[9] he said in one interview. "They just swam a better race than me, a smarter race than me, and were better prepared than me." No excuses. His fault. Facts. And within those facts were the answers to how he could win the next races: race smarter, prepare better, swim harder.

The other reality was how lousy he felt about the loss. "It's just really frustrating to start off on a bad note like this." He was used to winning, and losing on the brightest stage burned him. Denying that we feel bad when we fail or when catastrophe strikes isn't brave, it's dumb. If you're operating in denial, it's easy to miss important signs or to allow negative emotions to creep up on you.

But once he admits it, Phelps doesn't stay in that negative moment. He doesn't wallow. (Why would he? There was nothing he could do about the loss.) And he doesn't let his anger with himself turn into bad or irrational behavior. "The biggest thing now is to try to look forward," he said. He didn't let his wounded pride override his better judgment. He didn't make any grandiose statements. Instead, he saluted the winner, tweeting, "Congrats to @RyanLochte . . . Way to keep that title in the country where it belongs!" And Ryan Lochte responded with respect: "Thanks @MichaelPhelps I couldn't do it without you."

We don't know what happened out of the public eye, obviously, but Phelps's performance for the rest of the games is all the proof we need that he had the winning outlook.

Of course, it's also interesting that even the highest achievers—those who are totally committed, who pay the biggest price—can fall into incredibly bad behavior once they lose their focus and commitment. Like many people, he retired, exhausted after achieving his biggest goal. However, he didn't set a new goal or establish a new purpose. He didn't make an adjustment that would give him something big to channel his energy and competitive spirit. (I'll cover how to manage your momentum after a win in chapter 5.) The result has been embarrassment and a loss of reputation in the public eye. But now he is working it out, regaining his grip on reality, deciding what adjustments to make, and reconnecting with his winning drive.

DON'T LET EMOTION OVERRIDE REALITY

Life will send you a seemingly endless stream of annoyances, interruptions, and occasionally even some disasters. Don't allow yourself to be overwhelmed by emotion—even when it seems you're facing disaster.

Disasters are unpredictable. Sudden and shocking, they are lightening bolts striking from a clear blue sky. And when they hit us, we panic. We become irrational. We blow up the problem until it seems insurmountable. We hyper-focus on the potential devastation that could still occur. Our brains are hardwired to zero in on the danger or threats in our environment, so we lose touch with reality. And that's when quitting seems like the best option.

*When we disconnect from reality,
we don't make smart decisions.*

Are you letting yourself get rattled? If so, you're in danger of succumbing to a failing we all share: striking out or making rash decisions in the heat of the moment. When we let it, emotion can easily override logic.

Ephesians 4:26 states "Be angry and yet sin not." There's nothing wrong with getting angry. In fact, if you never really get angry, you probably aren't doing something that really matters to you. Anger comes when you aren't getting the results you want. The key is to use the anger to drive yourself to improve. However, if you get really wound up and you want to make a move because of the anger—you want to fire somebody, you want to tell your boss off, you want to write a scathing email to one of your partners—that's the moment to take control. Winners maintain perspective and don't make rash moves that they'll later regret—like quitting. Instead, they pay attention to what is making them angry and use this information to drive themselves forward in a positive way. Developing this discipline will stabilize you and will help you rebound faster from the low points.

A point of caution: Rash decisions can also be prompted by overwhelming positive emotions. Don't give in to euphoria. It can lead to outcomes equally as bad as those driven by anger.

Failures, setbacks, bad luck, disasters—they are there to serve you, not hold you back. They toughen you up and drive you to improve. Frustration fuels growth. It gives you the energy and resolve to clean yourself up, get organized, fix what you can, and take the next step.

This Too Shall Pass

Bad luck can kick off a cycle of negativity if we aren't on our guard. We focus on what went wrong and how we might have avoided it. Worse, we worry that it's a sign that we're on a path toward greater disaster. There's little point to obsessing about negative possibilities, yet people have struggled not to since the beginning of time. In the first century AD, Seneca said, "There are more things to alarm us than to harm us, and we suffer more often in apprehension than in reality." Simply put, 99 percent of the things you fear never happen.

What allows winners to maintain perspective is a deep, abiding truth: This too shall pass. When bad luck falls out of the sky and knocks you off your feet, remind yourself that it's temporary. It's a situation. It's a circumstance. It's a bump on the road, not the end of the road. "You mustn't confuse a single failure with a final defeat," wrote F. Scott Fitzgerald (it was uttered by a character in *Tender Is the Night*). It's not a sign of things to come. The current trial may even be a blessing in disguise, but the only way to find out is to keep moving forward.

Don't waste time worrying about what has gone wrong in the past or what *might* go wrong in the future. Reserve that mental and emotional energy to come up with a solution to the things that *actually* go wrong.

A Support System Can Help

Another truth about serial winners? They usually have a support system—people who keep them from quitting when they're on the edge. People who will help them see the facts and recognize when their emotions are taking center stage. It's a huge help to surround yourself with people who know what you're capable of and who have the big picture and your best interests at heart. They can give you the support and the reality therapy you need to toughen you up and keep you going when you get weak.

Our spouses are usually the first line of defense against a sudden desire to quit. The saving grace is when your spouse doesn't want you to quit the same day you want to. Richard, a friend in the company, once told me that every time he would have a tough day or week or quarter, he'd go home and gripe about all the things that were going wrong. His wife would listen quietly and then give him a sweet smile and say, "Well, you can always quit." She knew it would annoy him enough to get him refocused on how to improve the situation.

Another guy on our team hit a rough patch after a great start in the company. In one week, four of the five guys he recruited quit, and all the sales appointments he had gone on were nos. He came home fussing and fuming and said to his wife, "Things can't get any worse!"

"Well, actually they can," she replied. "While you were out, your last recruit called and quit."

"That's it! *I* quit!" he shouted. He ranted on for a while and when he had tired himself out, she said. "Okay, you go ahead and quit. Right now, go to bed and get some rest. Because in the morning, you're going to get your butt up and go right back at it because this business is the best chance we've ever had to have the life we want."

Serial winners are driven, positive, expectant, but not delusional.

They use their frustration to fuel a bounce back. They recognize that you'll never be handed more than the *opportunity* to achieve—we can influence results, but we can't control them. *They don't play the blame game.* They confront the truths, especially the hard ones. And then they turn their sights toward overcoming.

FOCUS ON THE PROBLEMS THAT ARE YOURS TO SOLVE

One of the most common ways we overcomplicate our lives or get trapped by problems is by trying to solve problems that aren't ours to solve. It's true, winners are overcomers. They attack problems. But they also don't worry about what they can't control. They focus on what is within their control, and that simplifies situations pretty quickly.

Are you overcomplicating a problem? Need a simple solution to get you unstuck? Follow the 90/10/5 rule.

90 percent of most things go smoothly.
10 percent will go haywire,
no matter what you do to prevent it.
Half of that, or 5 percent, is yours to deal with.

That 10 percent of a project or the steps toward a goal that go badly can consume all our energy and focus. But only half of any problem is either your fault or within your control. The other half is usually somebody else's responsibility or out of everyone's control. So why get upset about it? Perspective can save you a lot of unnecessary grief and keep you from making things worse than they are. You don't want to be the person who takes every molehill-sized problem and turns it into a mountain by overreacting.

Focus on the small percentage of the problems in your work or your projects that are within your control, do what you can to remedy them, and move on!

Ever heard of outlet stores? That's where retailers sell second quality goods (and goods that didn't sell at the regular stores). Why do they have to have specific stores for that purpose? Because no factory produces 100 percent quality. Instead of wasting time trying to eliminate all possible mistakes, they make the most of what they have and move on. In the "factory" of activity in your life you'll never achieve 100 percent either. You're not perfect. They're not perfect. Get over it. Move on.

Problems are like knots. If it's not your problem to solve, leave it to somebody else to untangle. If it is your problem to solve, know that there's not a knot out there that can't be untangled with enough patience. But be careful—they aren't all worth the trouble. The best thing you can do to reduce unnecessary frustration and maintain your perspective is to check in with reality: Is it somebody else's problem? Is it your problem and worth fixing? Or is it a problem that can't be fixed or isn't worth the effort? Don't be afraid of the hard work of problem-solving. But if you've wasted enough time on it and you aren't making any progress, maybe it's time to adjust and find a new path toward your next goal. Cut the problem out of your life entirely.

HAVE FAITH

Life is too big and complicated for you to handle on your own. This is a truth that all serial winners realize eventually. You're going to need help, a source of strength. You'll need something to sustain you in tough times. For me, my life and my world view are built upon my faith in God and the saving grace of the Lord Jesus Christ. Without that, I wouldn't have survived. You may have a different foundation. Whatever it is, make sure you give it the same energy and attention as everything else in your life, because there will come a time—and probably many times—when you need it.

If your foundation is different from mine, the rest of this section may not hold much meaning for you.

Mark Richt is the longtime football coach of the University of Georgia Bulldogs. I once read an interview with him in which he described the challenges of moving from the assistant coach position at Florida State to head coach. When he got the job, he had to immediately move so that he could assemble his team and staff. His wife stayed behind in Florida to make the arrangements for the move, sell the house, and let the kids finish out the school year. For several months he lived in a hotel by himself. He would find himself "face down on the floor of the Holiday Inn, asking God for the strength to go to work."[10] Of course, he found it and still relies on his faith. "What makes this job doable for me is that I rely completely on God for my strength. If I really try to do this job on my own power, it's just too big a job."[11] Richt has said that he tries to live according to Colossians 3:23: "And whatever you do, do heartily, as to the Lord and not to men."

I haven't always agreed with every decision Mark Richt has made as a football coach, but I can totally agree with his perspective on faith. In fact, I have gone through similar experiences at different stages in my career. I have felt called to do things that to me seemed totally impossible. The biggest one was to pursue a career in sales. My background was construction, and I used to tell people that it would have been easier for me to learn astrophysics in Russian than to learn how to sell anything. There were nights after yet another failed sales attempt when I would just have to laugh at how bad I was. I remember saying to the Lord, "If you can make me into a salesperson, that will be the greatest miracle of our generation." But over time that's exactly what he did. What I learned was that as long as I was willing, he would guide me and give me the power to learn what I needed to know.

It would be the easiest thing in the world to leave this part of my story out, but for me to pretend that I could have been successful without the strength of my faith would be hypocrisy.

You will be overwhelmed in life. You will run out of ideas

and energy. What are you going to do then? If you're trying to do something that the Lord wants you to do, he'll give you the strength and resources and insights to get it done. If you don't know what to do, call on the Lord and he'll guide you. If you fear you don't have the strength, call on the Lord and he'll provide it.

* * *

When difficulties arrive, winners don't allow themselves to be knocked back into the cocoon. They don't deny reality, they confront it. They let their frustration fuel their next steps forward. They maintain perspective on the problems they face. And they keep their faith. So take a breath, splash some cold water on your face, and start figuring out how to adjust to your new reality.

WINNING IS A SERIES OF ADJUSTMENTS

—

We adapt to the world; the world doesn't adapt to us.

But how do we do that? How do we get out of sticky situations? How do we make smart choices that will improve our chances of success?

Start with action, gather more input, simplify, and make small, regular adjustments.

ACTION = PROGRESS

Serial winners handle disasters the same way they handle success: they maintain their focus and keep moving forward. If you've had one disappointment or eight hundred, like Mark Ruffalo, you keep moving forward.

*Whenever disasters or bad luck
seem to kill your momentum,
immediately spring into action.*

What do you do? What action do you take? Well, first, consider your game plan. You developed it for a reason: It gives you a point of focus. What's the next step and what can you do now to get closer to it or complete it?

But what if your game plan has blown up? Then you turn to your alternate routes. "Action tests ideas," is a favorite saying of John Paul Caponigro, a photographer and artist. You don't know what results your plan will produce or what unexpected hurdles you'll face until you start. As you take each step, you learn. And as you learn, you begin to see the need and opportunity for alternate routes, what some people call backup plans.

Patrick Thean has launched and sold multiple companies, coaches multimillion-dollar companies on how to get things done and keep growing, and wrote *Rhythm: How to Achieve Breakthrough Execution and Accelerate Growth*. His advice to avoid getting stuck when a problem crops up? Develop a backup plan for "big stuff"—"that mega-important project that you cannot allow to fail . . . Consider your most critical-path projects, your most important milestones, and make sure you are prepared for an adjustment if it becomes necessary."[12]

Are you prepared to adjust if something big goes wrong? What if you start to run out of cash for your new business? What if the promotion you were counting on as the next step toward your big goal doesn't come through? Without one or two alternate routes, you may be in danger. That's why rock climbers have a rope that they secure at key points on the climbing route. If a climber loses his grip, the rope minimizes the danger. In the rock-climbing world, the most extreme are the free climbers, but even they have a rope.

It's hard to know where or when you might need an alternate route, but spend some time considering the most important aspects of your plan. Ask: What if I get to this point and my plan doesn't make sense anymore? What if the funds or support or progress I'm counting on don't come through? What else could I do to keep progressing toward the goal? As you win more and more, you'll develop better judgment and identify the most likely places where you may get hung up or identify the moments when you'll need to maintain forward movement no matter what.

It's like when I fly out of Aspen. I spend part of the year there, so I fly in and out of the airport quite a lot. I know that 25 percent of the time, my flight out will be canceled due to weather. I don't waste one second of time when it happens. If they say they aren't flying, I turn right around and call my office. I ask them to find another flight out from either Denver or Eagle-Vail. By the time I get to my car, drive out of Aspen and get to Interstate 70, I know which airport to drive to.

If you don't have an alternate route, do whatever comes to mind. Seriously. Doing something is almost always better than doing nothing. Focus on your target and on what you *can* do, and choose the best available option. Call a shot and keep moving. Why? First of all, action is the source of hope and the cure for most depression. (I'm talking about temporary depression here, not clinical.) You can go to anybody who is on the edge and say, "I know you want to give up, but isn't there one more thing you could do before you jump? Don't you want to do that first? Let's go do that." And with the thought of one action that could improve their situation, their whole dynamic changes. That's what winners know.

Serial winners stay in control by focusing on what they can do next and then doing it. Others lose control when they stop in their tracks and let their imaginations keep them from taking action.

Second, and it always comes back to this simple point, the way to move from survival to success is one inch at a time. If you can't run, you walk. If you can't walk, you crawl. Eventually you'll be able to stand, to walk, to jog, and then to run again. It's a fact that you can't go from being knocked flat to running in a single breath. You'll need time to recover, to clear your head. But you keep moving forward, even if it's slowly at first. Because at the end of the day real knowledge comes from activity.

FACTS = COMPETITIVE EDGE

You're probably familiar with the acronym GIGO: garbage in, garbage out. It's popular in the computer industry because it captures the problem of user error so succinctly. The process of decision-making is a lot like computer processing. If you have bad information, guess what will happen? You'll make bad decisions—bad adjustments—and get bad results. If you're getting bad outcomes, maybe you need to improve the input.

Serial winners go after the answers they need and they stay informed to improve their decision-making.

Winners are curious. They want to know enough about what's happening, about current trends, and about new innovations to evaluate what they hear from the grapevine or the media. They know you don't get ahead in life by following half-truths, worn out theories, or trends that are past their peak. Donald Trump gets up at 5:00 a.m. every day. It's time-consuming to stay informed. He reads stacks of newspapers, cuts out relevant articles, and passes them on to his staff for follow-up. He thinks it gives him an advantage, and it does.

A friend of mine who is a doctor told me that he reads medical journals in his specialty for at least an hour every day. At that rate, it would take him one hundred years to read the research that is published in just a single year. That doesn't matter. He devotes as much time as he can because it's the price of staying informed about research, treatments, and technology.

Develop a system for staying informed. It's a lot of effort but winners know to stay on top you have to do it. In the real world, if you don't stay current on the facts of what's happening in your industry, you will be run over by those who do.

Hunt Down the Answers You Need

When winners run into problems, they don't stall out, waiting for answers to fall into their laps. If they don't already know what they need to do, they immediately begin turning over every rock looking for answers until they get one they can use. Losers don't do that. When they run into a problem, they immediately slip out of gear, idling in place as they wonder, "Am I good enough? Should I be doing this? Is this a mistake? Is this the right time? Winners frame the issue: What is it I want to do? Is it possible? How quick can I make it happen? What's the surest way around this obstacle?"

Where can you find the information you need? Um . . . everywhere? One of the greatest benefits of the modern era is access to information. It's everywhere—tons of free or cheap information from experts in your field, including people who have faced the exact problem you face right now. And it's all available to anybody who's not too lazy to look for it. Start online. Read interviews with the best and brightest. Join forums. Read books about the particular challenge you're facing or by leaders you've come to respect. If you need to adapt quickly, there's enough information available immediately to give you a good list of options.

Talk to people who are doing well and get some fresh input. Explain what you've tried to do and why you think it's not working. Ask them for their opinion or for any stories of how they've overcome similar challenges. And don't ignore those closest to the situation or those directly involved. They have the most information and the best instincts. Ask for their input. Even if you don't agree with their conclusions, you need to know what they are thinking and why.

If you've taken a hit and you're stuck, frame the issue. Gather the facts. Do your research. Focus on what you know, and not all the unknowns. Once you have enough information to make a reasonably well-informed decision (remember, don't get stuck in the research stage!), unemotionally clarify your choices. Eliminate the obviously bad or truly impossible. Consider the best options, implement them, and then continue to simplify.

SIMPLICITY = SPEED

Google controls 68 percent of the search-engine market as I'm writing this. That's massive market share. And they got there fast. They hit 60 percent market share just seven years after they launched in 1998. Many experts credit Google's flight to the top with the simplicity of their search page. The word "Google," an empty field, and almost nothing else. The simplicity was accidental to begin with. Sergey Brin and Larry Page were coders and engineers, not web designers. Brin didn't even really know HTML. So they did as little as possible to create a page that connected with the back-end technology. Eventually, they saw the wisdom in the accident.

From that point forward, Brin and Page guarded the value they had found in the simplicity. In 2005, Marissa Mayer was director of web products at Google and was described this way in an article: "She's also Google's high priestess of simplicity, defending the home page against all who would clutter it up. 'I'm the gatekeeper,' she says cheerfully. 'I have to say no to a lot of people.'"[13] Today, the product engineers and designers have to fight and win many heroic battles to get their new feature, word, or idea added to the main search page. Keeping things as simple as possible paid off big for Google.

The difference between complicated and simple is often the difference between winning and losing. If you have hit a hurdle or aren't making the progress you want or have been hit by some disaster, it's likely that you've either made things overly complicated or complications have been thrust upon you.

The best way forward is to fight to keep things simple—and it will be a fight.

Serial winners know that simplicity and speed go hand in hand. If it's complicated, it takes more skill, more time, or more training. We have more things to keep up with and more things can go wrong. When we're stuck or moving slow, we need ideas for making progress that are efficient and can be implemented quickly. We need simple adaptations and simple solutions. We need a simple route forward or around an obstacle.

One of my favorite scenes from *Raiders of the Lost Ark* is when Harrison Ford is trying to rescue Karen Allen, who has been carried off in a basket by the evil Nazis. He escapes or fights his way through villain after villain at a street market in a chaotic and complicated series of events. He thinks he's in the clear when an Arab swordsman with a scimitar pops up in his path and shows off his impressive skills in a dazzling swirl of maneuvers. Ford watches him, waiting until he's finished, knowing he has no chance to win this sword fight, and then pulls out his gun and shoots him. Problem solved.

If you want to limit the number of problems you encounter entirely, continue to simplify your plan as you learn and grow. The simpler you keep it, the faster you'll progress. And when you're struggling to overcome an obstacle, consider the simplest options first. Start there. Don't make anything more complicated than you need to—until you need to.

SMALL ADJUSTMENTS = CONSISTENT GROWTH

Adjustments are about staying on track and maintaining your pace. If you're on the highway and your lane suddenly slows down, you switch lanes, right? It's a small, simple adjustment. Small, simple, regular adjustments are the key to consistent growth and progress.

Serial winners rely on small adjustments to reduce the natural human resistance to change. We all resist change, so don't try to deny it. There are very few people in the world who feel comfortable with change, especially big change. And sometimes we feel stuck *because* we're resisting the big change we need to make. Unfortunately the longer we delay, the farther off course or off pace we get, and the bigger adjustment it takes to get us back on track or up to speed. One of the best ways to avoid the need for an overwhelming adjustment is to make smaller changes when we can and when we should.

Small changes also keep you from developing ruts. At work, if your goal is to head up a group or a team, maybe you regularly volunteer for different task forces, ask for a new responsibility or two, or spend some time researching solutions to some of the problems that the team might face. Make small adjustments that help you grow into the opportunity you want.

Sometimes in life, though, we get diverted or our attention

drifts. What might once have been a small problem has suddenly become a big problem, even an emergency. That's when you're going to have to make a big adjustment to get yourself back on track. Other times, something out of the blue happens that requires you to make a big, bold adjustment and fast. But most of the time, progress and success are about small adjustments. When you add up all the fine-tuning serial winners do over a week, a month, or a year to overcome the series of small hurdles life puts in our way, you'll see incredible improvements.

At any moment, you could be just one small adjustment away from a major success. If you can find a way to get a bit more organized, push yourself a little harder, bring another degree of focus to your work or goal, you might make it past the plateau or the obstacle and speed forward across the finish line.

* * *

No one wins all the time, but we can fight to win all the time. The easiest thing to do when we hit a wall is to slack off, to rationalize, to settle, to make excuses, to blame others. The hardest person to manage is yourself. But if you're going for something you really want, you'll fight for it. You'll overcome any obstacle in your path. It's the only way to win.

THE
CYCLE
OF
WINNING

1 DECIDE

2 OVERDO

3 ADJUST

4 FINISH

5 KEEP IMPROVING

CHAPTER 4

DON'T JUST START, FINISH

It's moving day. You've spent the past nine months working with a developer to build a new house, and it's finally done. The movers have loaded your furniture onto the truck, the whole family is in the car, and you're pulling into your new driveway.

Immediately, you sense something is wrong. There's a pile of debris next to the house. Your spouse says, "That shouldn't be there." You take a breath and think, "It's fine. No big deal." The kids pile out and run to the porch, so excited to see their new bedrooms. You follow, unlock the front door, and walk into your new castle.

Uh-oh.

The painters haven't finished in the living room. In the kitchen, you find that the sink hasn't been installed yet. Most of the electrical outlets don't have plates over them. Upstairs, the baseboards haven't been installed in the bathroom and closet doors haven't been hung in the bedrooms.

Now it's a big deal. *The house isn't finished.*

You call the supervisor for the project and explain what you've found in the calmest voice you can muster. "Oh, I'm sorry," he replies. "We intended to do it. We've worked really hard. Our team is well trained. We usually get houses done by the move-in date."

Which of his excuses makes the failure acceptable to you?

None!

You don't care that they tried. You don't care that they usually meet deadlines. You don't care about their team. What you care about is your excited family and a truckload of furniture with nowhere to go.

Straight out of college, I became a supervisor for a home developer. I soon understood what people meant when they said, "It seems like it takes 98 percent of the effort to get the last 2 percent done." And deadlines take on a new meaning when you've got a family showing up to move in on a certain date. Every last loose end needs to be resolved by that date. No excuses! But in the last two weeks, the problems that arise seem almost insurmountable—like the time the plumber tracked mud across the newly installed white shag carpet (this was the '70s, after all) as the moving van rounded the corner.

Every August we would have two or three families per week pulling up with their eighteen-wheelers full of furniture, ready to move into their new dream home. You know the funny thing? Not one of them cared about what was going on at the other houses. The only house they cared about was theirs. And if it wasn't ready, they would unleash the fury. It was my job to finish their house, on time, no excuses. The only alternative was losing a customer, money, our sense of pride in our work, our reputation in the industry, or all of the above.

Every project you work on is the same. Whether it's making sales numbers for the quarter or pulling off your kid's circus-themed birthday party, *somebody is counting on you to finish*. The people we hold in high opinion, the people we trust, and the people we follow are the people who can be counted on to get it done, whatever *it* is.

Finishing is how you earn the great things in life—trust, respect, loyalty, opportunity, even money.

If you can't be counted on, nobody will take you seriously. Your training won't matter. Your contacts and friends and

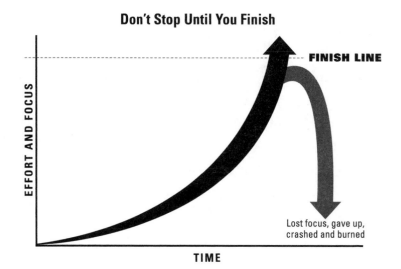

Don't Stop Until You Finish

FINISH LINE

EFFORT AND FOCUS

Lost focus, gave up,
crashed and burned

TIME

network of relationships won't matter. Your likeability factor won't matter. Because those don't erase the inability to get things done.

Yes, it can be difficult to make it the last 2 percent of the journey, which is why so many people bail out when they are just shy of their goal. Serial winners resist the temptation to give up and give in. That last push before the finish line is a time for focus and toughness, not weakness. They know that what you could have done, what you intended to do, or what you worked at for a long time don't matter.

To win, you have to finish.

Winners establish their worth (they win) by producing, and the only way to produce results is to finish what you start.

ALMOST FINISHED GETS YOU ALMOST NOTHING

—

It plays out in front of us almost every day. One person rises to the occasion while another falls.

The pressure is on, and when it absolutely matters, one person makes it happen. She makes the shot, pulls off the project, makes the deadline. That ability is her trump card in life. It elevates her.

Ninety-eight percent done isn't done, even though a lot of us like to think it is. Winners cover the last 2 percent because they know it's the best way to pull ahead of the pack—the talkers. And until you get the job done—all the way done—that's all you are. A talker. The world is full of people who almost finish. We don't need more of them. We need more people who close the gap between 98 and 100 percent. We lose and the world loses when we bail out at 98.

The world needs more finishers.

Winners know how good it feels to accomplish a goal, and they *want* that goal. They know they can't count on anybody else to make it happen. If they fail to finish, everything they've gone through to get as far as they have will have been for nothing, and everything they might have learned or discovered by finishing will have been lost.

THE DANGERS OF FAILING TO FINISH

In the last chapter, I wrote a lot about quitting. Usually, quitting is a bad idea. A really bad idea. At certain points—say, early in a project if you find you're just not that committed—you might recover. It may be a necessary adjustment. But quitting when you're 98 percent of the way there? That's a disaster.

If you quit when you're close to the finish line, you lose the full return on your investment of time, energy, effort, and money.

All the time. All the money. All the thinking, the planning, the working. All gone. Wasting those resources is a big hit.

When I lived in North Carolina, we owned a horse farm. Riding competitively was becoming our family activity, and we were buying one horse after another. Well, we needed a way to water the horses and hoses weren't cutting it. So we decided to have a well dug. We assumed that a 100-foot well would get us access to the small amount of water we needed. We hired surveyors to come out and identify the best spot to drill. We hired a good drilling company and set the date. They showed up, drilled the agreed-upon 100 feet. No water.

They turned to me and asked, "Do you want us to keep digging?"

I knew if we went deeper the bill was going to go higher, but I had to pay them for the drilling they had already done, so . . . "Okay, let's go another 100 feet." I was sure that we would hit something before then.

Nope.

"Should we keep going?"

"Fine," I muttered.

They drilled to 300 feet, and then 400 feet. Still no water. At this point we were starting to assume the farm was sitting on top of the Sahara Desert. But what was I going to do? Was I really going to stop? I would have to pay these guys for a 400-foot well that wasn't producing any water.

So we kept going. At 420 feet they hit a mighty river. We

had so much water we could have supplied the county. Nobody would have blamed us for stopping at 400 feet, but if we had, all that work and investment would have been lost. And we still wouldn't have been able to water the horses!

At the time I was reminded of Napoleon Hill's "Three Feet from Gold" story from *Think and Grow Rich* (Alba & Tromm, 2010). I never expected to have such a clear-cut example of it in my own life. It certainly cemented the lesson for me.

Failing to finish leaves you high and dry. Worse, it damages your reputation. You don't get anything big done on your own. It takes the support of your team, your partners, your network, your family, even your community. When you fail to finish, they notice. When you try to rally them to support your next project, they'll roll their eyes and say, "Yeah, we've been down this road before. Fool us once . . ." You'll have a hard time rebuilding your reputation and gaining the support you need to win if you don't prove to people that you know how to finish.

Finally, if you give up and slide back down, you'll damage your confidence. It's one thing for others to give up on you. The real damage comes when you start doubting yourself. You'll have to find something else to get excited about, but it will be harder to build the energy and momentum to succeed because you have to overcome the mental baggage of quitting on yourself. And that's when quitting can start to become a very bad habit.

THE BENEFITS OF ACTUALLY FINISHING

Let's say that you really love to cook. You've had a little experience outside of your own kitchen, but not much. Still, you decide that you're going to try out for a cooking show. "Why not?" you say to yourself. "I don't care if I'm the first one kicked off. I just want to prove that I can qualify and compete." You apply, you try out, you make it to the next level, you cook for more judges, you go through more interviews. It takes months. But you keep at it. Just when you think you don't have much more effort or time to give to this goal, you get the word that you're on the show! Fantastic. You rearrange your life to head off to the filming location for the six weeks it takes to film the show. You arrive and are overwhelmed by the experience and talent of the other contestants. The first cooking challenge arrives and it's tough. Really tough.

You may win, or you may be one of the first off the show. Would you be disappointed? Sure. But you would get over it quickly because you would have achieved exactly what you set out to achieve. No matter the result, you still come out a big winner. You spent time with other talented professionals, your overall skill level probably improved, and the exposure could bring new opportunities you might never have had.

Most important, though, is that you've proven to yourself that you can finish.

Finishing is a moment of truth for winners.

Finishing Gives You Confidence

Confidence is the belief that no matter what happens, you'll find a way. Recall the discussion of confidence from chapter 2: The best form of confidence is the confidence that comes from achievement—from finishing what we start. Because confidence is the belief that no matter what happens, you'll find a way.

Until you finish and prove to yourself and the world that you can, there will always be questions. You'll have doubts about yourself—we all do. Others will doubt you. No one thinks you can do big things—until you do them. Finishing is your opportunity to prove your worth, to prove that you can be counted on, to prove your faith, to prove that you're more than just talk. The benefits of proving yourself to yourself and to the world are long-term and far-reaching.

Learning how to get things done, especially within a specific timeframe, is all about problem-solving. The more experience you have in solving problems, the more efficient you become and the more confidence you have when facing a problem. You learn when to ask for help and who to ask. You learn how to leverage the resources available to you. You learn how to build a team. You learn how to find alternative routes to get to the end.

The more capable you feel, the less likely you are to slip into poor-me thinking.

Finishing Expands Your Vision

After pro golfer Bubba Watson won his first Masters tournament in 2012, he was interviewed in the Butler Cabin, where the tradition of the green jacket takes place. (The previous year's winner bestows the new champion with a green suit jacket.) One journalist asked Watson if winning the Masters was a dream come true. What he said captured a major truth about achieving a goal: "I've never had a dream go this far, so I can't really say it's a dream come true."[14] Most of us don't even know what we're capable of achieving, or what could be possible beyond our dreams. And we'll never know until we finish at least our first big goal. Bubba's dream was to become a professional golfer. Until he achieved that, nothing that came after was possible.

Every time you finish, it's like you've reached the top of a hill. Until you get to the top, you don't know what's on the other side. Once you do, you can see all the opportunities and options. Because you finished the first thing, you have the confidence to go for new things you had never considered before or that you didn't even know were possible until you did the first thing. If you never finish your first goal, who knows what you might be giving up.

Finishing Small Things Helps You Build a Pattern

Finishing the big things matters, but the little things matter too. If you can't do the little things, you'll never develop the strength of will to do the big things. If you say you're going to buy a classic French cookbook and make two recipes out of it every week, you do it. If you say you're going to get on the treadmill for twenty minutes every night, you do it. If you say you're going to spend an hour every week improving a leadership skill, you do it. If you say you're going to attend two industry networking events a month, you do it. You commit. Because winning isn't a one-time thing, it's an all the time thing. To keep winning, you have to keep producing in all areas of your life, even if what you're producing is growth in your abilities. You build a pattern: I finish, I finish, I finish.

Jerry Seinfeld developed a great approach for keeping himself accountable for achieving his daily goals. Brad Isaac, a young comic, asked Seinfeld for advice, and this is what Seinfeld told him: To be a better comic, you need better jokes. The only way to have better jokes is to keep writing them. But it can be hard to stick to a goal of writing every day. Seinfeld told Isaac to get a wall calendar and a red magic marker. Every day he completed his writing goal, he should put a big X through that date. Day by day, he would create a chain of Xs. The chain would get longer. His whole focus should be on *not breaking the chain.*

Isaac took Seinfeld's advice. Each day, he finished. The chain got longer. His jokes got better. More important, though, is that Isaac started using the system in other areas of his life, to achieve other goals. This simple approach helped him develop a pattern of finishing, which led to bigger and bigger things.

It doesn't matter what technique you use. (I used something called an activity jar when building my business.) What matters is that you develop the pattern. Our problem-solving, creative, future-focused thinking happens in the prefrontal cortex. It has limited capacity. Our habits are run out of our basal ganglia. The more activity we can push to that part of the brain, the more mental capacity we have to spend on solving new problems, tackling new challenges, and getting ourselves across the finish line.

> *With each new achievement the benefits compound. You become stronger, wiser, and more capable of winning in the future.*

What is it you need to commit to doing? What small goals do you need to finish daily, weekly, or monthly to keep you on track for your bigger goals? How will you develop a pattern of finishing?

To Get Paid, You Have to Finish

Bottom line: in business, you can't get paid if you can't produce. Whether you're running your own business or working for somebody else, the people who progress in their careers, who build strong businesses, and who make more money are the people who produce better results. And that means finishing the job, time after time!

Business is a competition, and when you're competing, you must produce. You must put numbers on the board. The numbers are your credentials—proof of your abilities and worth to a team or organization. We don't get paid to talk about producing, to make plans for producing, to prepare to produce, or to train others on how to produce. The biggest rewards, in career advancement and money, go to the people who actually produce.

Winners make themselves rare and valuable by what they accomplish, and that will never change.

* * *

Nobody's perfect; nobody wins every time. It's true that unforeseeable disasters can derail us, and sometimes we derail ourselves. The payoff—in personal growth, in fulfillment, and in money—comes from actually finishing the job, though, so you need to finish a lot more often than you don't. Just don't be surprised if it gets a little tough at the end.

MENTAL TOUGHNESS AND
THE LAST 2 PERCENT

—

Winning is like climbing the tallest mountains.

To get started, you have to expend a lot of energy and resources—training, gear, coaching, trips to practice on increasingly higher mountains. Your passion to be one of the few to climb the tallest mountains drives you on. Once you begin to build some experience, each climb becomes more natural and your progress becomes steadier. Finally, you're ready. You decide to go for it. Everest.

You plan the trip. You pay the fees. You trek for seven days just to reach Base Camp I. And then you begin the real climb. It takes weeks, hiking and climbing 12.5 miles—if you take the short route. Slowly you dispatch one phase after another, step by step. Every day, you're a few hundred feet higher. Your training serves you well. Finally, you break 26,000 feet and cross over into the Death Zone—the altitude above which you will likely die if you aren't using supplemental oxygen. Not long after, you reach Base Camp VI, the final base camp. From here, you'll make your last push for the summit.

The closer you get to the top, the thinner the air becomes. The temperature drops. The wind speeds increase. The possibility of rescue becomes a fantasy. The possibility of death becomes a reality. And you know that the longer you take, the more likely it is you won't reach the summit—or get back to base camp.

Do you think once climbers begin the final push, they start thinking, "Well, I've done the hard work. From here it should be a cakewalk"? No, of course not. Thinking like that will get them killed.

There is no better analogy for winning. No, not many goals you set require you to literally risk your life. But every goal does require you to risk resources, energy, happiness, and progress toward other goals. Most of us take those risks every day. We decide on a goal, are gung-ho in the beginning and give it a lot of energy. We establish a pattern and maintain steady forward progress. We fight until we're just a few feet away. And then . . .

Let's not pretend. Just like water flows downhill and follows the path of least resistance, the default operating mode of human beings is to make excuses when things get tough—and things always get tough at the end. We'd like to think that the natural thing is to buckle down and find a way to win, despite what happens, but that's not usually how it goes.

To overcome our default thinking, we need mental toughness—that will to win that kicks in at the toughest times and drives you to shut up, stay focused, and keep fighting until you finish.

Three things cause our mental toughness to disappear right when we need it the most:

- overconfidence in the momentum we've generated from previous successes,

- the mistaken belief that we've surpassed all the hurdles, and

- exhaustion.

What makes the last 2 percent seem so hard is that we expect it to be easy! We expect our momentum to carry us the rest of the way. We're mentally unprepared for the effort required to make it to the top—the same level of consistent effort and focus it took to cover the first 98 percent. Our expectations are skewed and we are vulnerable. It helps to know in advance that the ending will test you, because the only way to cross the finish line is to maintain our will to win.

SERIAL WINNERS DON'T COUNT ON PAST ACCOMPLISHMENTS

On January 21, 2007, the Indianapolis Colts' victory over the New England Patriots was the biggest come-from-behind win in any AFC Championship Game. At half time, the Patriots were ahead 21–3. They had it. They just needed to keep doing what they had been doing. But it all started to fall apart. The Colts scored 18 points in about twenty seconds! With just a couple of minutes left, the Patriots were still in the lead, but then Peyton Manning moved the ball all the way down the field for a final touchdown with just a few seconds left on the clock. The final score was Colts 38, Patriots 34. I think you can imagine how much fun the Colts had on the plane ride home.

I remember watching Patriots' coach Bill Belichick pacing on the sidelines shouting, "Finish the game! Finish the game!" But the Patriots couldn't. They allowed themselves to believe that achieving an early lead was enough. It was subconscious and none of them would admit it, but the results said they slacked off and let themselves get beaten. Every expert who watched the game said their offense wilted in the second half. Sure, they were exhausted, but so is every team in the last quarter. They knew they couldn't use that excuse.

Getting to 98 percent means that you've achieved a series of smaller wins already. You don't get that far without doing a lot of things right. And that's great. You're developing a pattern of winning. But past successes can sabotage you if you're not careful! You start to believe that the win is guaranteed. This is how great teams lose. This is how even successful people suddenly lose.

When you're in the last 2 percent, it doesn't matter what you've already accomplished. The only thing that matters is whether or not you finish.

You have to keep your head down and push forward until the game is over, until you've reached 100 percent. You have to fight the feeling of entitlement. You have to put a stop to thoughts like "I deserve this" or "Look at how hard I've worked to get here." It doesn't matter how smart, how prepared, or how talented you are. The end will be bitterly hard if you expect it to get easier. As tennis great Björn Borg once said, "Fight until the last ball. My list of matches shows that I have turned a great many so-called irretrievable defeats into victories."[15]

SERIAL WINNERS LIMIT NEGATIVE
STRESS WHENEVER POSSIBLE

There's a phrase I heard a while back and it immediately stuck in my head. "Carry your energy with you." No matter where you go, who you run into, or what challenge pops up, stay in control. Maintain your focus and positive attitude. Don't let yourself fall apart.

Like me, you may like that idea in theory, but find it tough to practice, especially when you've been working long and hard for something. You can become worn out and worn down. You may be physically exhausted. More important, you may have exhausted your willpower—a critical factor of mental toughness. For years, psychological studies have been proving that willpower can be depleted. If you have kids, think about how difficult they become in the hours just before bedtime. Their willpower is exhausted and they struggle to show the self-discipline you would really love to see at the time of day when your willpower, your patience, is exhausted too! As adults, our willpower can be depleted by stress, lack of sleep, lack of exercise, poor diet—all things that can occur when we're in the final push.

Winners help sustain their mental toughness by doing what they can to limit negative stress. They don't obsess over what might happen. They focus on what they should and can do right now. They resist the temptation to let emotion override logic. They use their ability to overcome and maintain their faith. They apply their self-discipline to their health and personal life so that they have the strength they need to finish. And this helps maintain their levels of willpower and grit. For many years, I put together conferences for Primerica team members. They were usually three-day affairs with speakers, special events, awards ceremonies for hundreds or (more often) thousands of people. People would travel hundreds of miles to attend. The conferences were a lot of fun and very productive. But they also took a lot of work. Every one was a complicated project—a lot like putting together a jigsaw puzzle. The pieces didn't always fit together exactly as we thought they would. But no matter what catastrophe emerged at the last minute, the show had to go on. Invariably, these "catastrophes" would begin falling out of the sky after noon on Wednesday, when the event was scheduled to begin at noon on Friday. Guest speakers would get the details wrong and fly into another town in another state. Oops! Awards weren't ready or the award company had put the wrong names on the wrong plaques. An hour before the doors were scheduled to open, you'd discover that the stagehands had set up the stage on the wrong side of the room or three-thousand chairs were facing the wrong direction.

After doing this for years and seeing a new "catastrophe" at every conference, I decided to save my mental health by developing a philosophy for my staff and meeting planners. After Wednesday at noon, no matter what happened, no matter how big the disaster, our reaction was, "Faaaaantastic! That will just make it better!" Half the attendees have the flu? Great, the rest of us will have more room. Guest speaker canceled? Great, it will give the rest of the speakers more time and they'll probably need it. By reducing our stress—our response to a situation, which is totally within our control—we were freed up to make the best adjustment we could and then move on with full energy. We never had a lesser event because of something that went wrong at the last minute.

We are most vulnerable *before* we've actually proven that we're capable of doing something big. In those moments we have to calm our minds, control our emotions, and tell ourselves, "I may not have done it before, but all I can do right now is move forward just a little bit farther." Winners don't allow themselves to be overwhelmed by last-minute, exasperating challenges. They don't lose focus and waste energy at critical moments. They overcome the hurdles and keep moving forward.

So the next time you're in the 2-percent zone and a problem crops up, say to yourself, "Faaaantastic! That will just make the finish better!" Letting it stress you out will just diminish your willpower and mental toughness.

SERIAL WINNERS STAY ON HIGH ALERT

Even though it was forty years ago, I can still remember how it felt when I was in the last few days of any building project. I would be so worn out, working eighty-hour weeks to complete a big development. I didn't want one more thing to deal with. Of course, something would happen—usually something simple, like the plumber tracking mud all the way across the brand-new, freshly installed white carpet. It wasn't that hard to solve (call some people and arrange to have it cleaned). It was just an additional strain at a point when I didn't feel I had a lot left to give.

The end of the process of winning is no different from any other part of the process—problems are going to crop up. The only difference is that now you're more vulnerable to poor-me thinking that can lead to quitting because you're worn out from the effort of getting this far. A last-minute problem can feel like the last straw. What do serial winners do? They stay on high alert. They turn over every stone, think through every last step, explore every vulnerability, and check and recheck to avoid being derailed at the last minute.

Serial winners think ahead to avoid being blindsided.

They know they're vulnerable, but they don't let themselves become more vulnerable by being unaware or unprepared. Players for the New England Patriots hate to be on the receiving end of one of Bill Belichick's famous questions. He drills them about the opponent. Who are the most dangerous players? How was their performance in the last three games? What are their weaknesses? Do they have families? Who did they play for before? Where did they play in college? What are the team's favorite plays? Which plays are most often successful? He is on high alert, and he expects his players to be there too. In an article in *The Wall Street Journal*, Heath Evans, a former fullback for the Patriots, said, "There's no limit to the knowledge Bill expects you to have on an opponent and the craziest part is he has the answers to all of it."[16] But the Patriots are generally acknowledged as the best-prepared team in the NFL. It doesn't guarantee that they'll win every time, but they sure win a lot.

When you get close to the finish line, everything becomes more critical, even the smallest details. What do you do the night before your third interview for your dream job? Do you go out partying with your friends? No! You stay in. You make sure your best suit is back from the dry cleaner. You read even more about the company. You read the bios of every person you're going to meet with the next day. You stalk them on LinkedIn. You think up thirty questions they might ask and carefully think through your answers. You do everything you can to solve any problems before they arise and to prepare, prepare, prepare.

Take finishing seriously. Leverage your mental toughness to get yourself to code red. Don't let yourself be blindsided.

* * *

Serial winners don't handle the end of a project the same way they handle the middle. The end is more like the beginning. They know they will be more vulnerable, more tired, more nervous. They keep these realities in mind to help them maintain perspective. They don't *let* themselves be beat. They put their heads down and climb until they reach the summit.

ABILITY × EFFORT, TALENT × FIGHT

—

The quicker we accept the fact that
winning isn't easy, the better.

Here's reality: Winning comes at a price. The price is hard work. Consistent effort over time. How much effort? Enough to get results. You work and fight your way forward. That's it. You don't stop until you get there. If you want to move up faster, you work even harder. You know you've done enough when you get the job done. Until it's done, you haven't done enough.

Effort and fight activate all your advantages—experience, talent, knowledge, skills. Those advantages are useless to you until you get to work and use them. It makes them come alive. I think of it like a mathematical equation:

Ability and Talent × *Effort and Fight* = *Winning Combination*

Unless hopelessly overmatched in ability or talent, greater effort and fight usually win the day. This explains the mystery of why the better team or player doesn't always win. Just because they *should* win doesn't mean they *will* win. It's why you have to get in there and play the game—on a given day, anything can happen.

Let's say you have two teams. You rate each team's ability and talent on a scale of 1 to 10 and you score their effort and fight as a percentage. How talented are they compared to others? Are they giving 70 percent or 80 percent? The comparison might look like this.

TEAM A		TEAM B
(Ability and Talent × Effort and Fight)	<	(Ability and Talent × Effort and Fight)
(8 × 60%) = 4.8		(6 × 90%) = 5.4

Who's going to win? Team B. They have lesser ability and talent, but they make up for it by working harder and wanting it more. And since no team or person consistently performs at

100 percent (even winners have moments of weakness), we can always find opportunities to beat the unbeatable.

Winners fight, they don't just hope. They don't hold back, believing that their talents and other advantages will carry them through. And winners work at winning every day, every moment, until they do. *Grinding* is one of the code words people use to describe how they achieve great things. It's not glamorous or sexy. It's not what you necessarily want to do. But it's what winners do.

Flying back from Chicago to New York on the team plane after a crushing playoff loss to the Chicago Bears, New York Giants coach Bill Parcells was as low as he had ever been. In an interview for the NFL Network series *A Football Life* after he was inducted into the NFL Hall of Fame, he recounted how this became a turning point.[17] Sitting next to him on the ride home was Mickey Corcoran, Bill's old high-school basketball coach who had worked with him as an advisor. Breaking the tension, Mickey leaned over to Bill and said, "Hey, Parcells, you've got to figure out a way to beat those guys." Bill might have exploded at any one else but since it was Mickey, he just said, "They're pretty good." Mickey replied, "Pretty good? They're magnificent. You've *still* got to figure out a way to beat those guys." Parcells called that moment a "head snapper." He forgot about the loss and locked in on figuring out a way to beat Chicago. That moment changed his career.

Effort and fight—determination, bulldog tenacity—are

the only things you can control. Yes, you can work to improve your abilities, and you should (we'll get into that in the next chapter). But in each moment, and particularly once you're in the 2-percent zone, you have the ability you have. At this point, if you're struggling to finish, your only option is to increase your effort and determination. Double down. Hang tough and get it done. Since you'll pay a price, win or lose, you might as well win.

When you've chased a dream and come up short, advice from every side will come in, urging you to slack off just when you're about to make your breakthrough. Because to others, your determination and fight might look hopeless. Don't listen to them. They mean well, but it's exactly the wrong advice! There will be plenty of time to rest later, and only you know what winning is worth to you. When it's harvest time, farmers hardly sleep. When a football team is marching for a game-winning touchdown, no one is thinking about how tired they are. When you get close to something you've worked hard for, for years, you don't back off until you get it done.

PREPARE FOR LUCK

We all know them. People who happened to be in the right place at the right time to capitalize on the next "big thing." People who met the right person at just the right moment in their lives to help them finally finish. People who stumble into great opportunities. People who release their ideas right when the world is eagerly awaiting them. The lucky ones.

They fall into success early. They leapfrog the menial jobs, the long hours, and the years of slow progress most of us suffer through. They're surrounded by supportive people on all sides—a helpful spouse, cooperative children, a crack staff, perfect business partners. Oil wells spring up in their backyards. If a tornado tears through town, it skips right over their houses. No matter what happens, everything they touch seems to turn to gold. Finishing for them is easy because they don't face the same hurdles we all face right at the end.

Sure, this sounds a bit extreme. But so is the number of people who believe in the myth of luck. Test me. Go out and ask thirty random people to list the top five contributors to big success. I bet most of them include luck. The truth?

Winners make their own luck through hard work and preparation.

People get "lucky" because they make it possible for "luck" to find them. They aren't at home on the couch, waiting for something great to happen. No. They have gone out into the world, committed to a goal, and have worked extremely hard for a long time to achieve it. They don't give up and they don't give in. It's that unnoticed hard work and perseverance that positioned them to capitalize on the good fortune that came their way. Luck is like catching a wave while surfing. You can't surf without the wave, but you can't take advantage of the wave until you

- get a board,

- get in the ocean at the right time of day,

- paddle out into position (which takes an incredible amount of work),

- keep your eye out for the right kind of incoming swells,

- choose a wave and start paddling like crazy to build your own momentum before the wave just washes over your head, and

- move into position as the wave crests and then dive in and ride it as far as you can and as long as you can.

At the end of a successful day of surfing, you might look around and tell everyone, "I was lucky. There were some great waves today." Right on! But you still had to be prepared to take advantage of them. That's how luck works.

Yes, lucky breaks do come along. Fairly often, in fact. A situation suddenly shifts and, behold, a life-changing opportunity or solution is revealed! You might call these *breaks* because winners keep applying pressure until the walls between them and their goals break down into rubble. They attack the situation every way they know how, until something finally gives or they find the weak spot. Voilà—a lucky break! It's not the final crumbling of the wall that really matters, though. The hard work of breaking it down is what prepares the winner to take that opportunity as far as it can go—toward bigger things.

Winner's win not *because* of lucky breaks. Lucky breaks take them the last 1 percent of the distance to the finish line. Winners win because they keep pushing and fighting until they do.

So many top comedians had their "big break" on *The Tonight Show* with Johnny Carson. Many of them have pointed to that moment and to Johnny Carson as the source of their success. Johnny always deflected the compliments, essentially saying that all he did was give them a five-minute spot on the show. They were the ones who went up there and knocked it out of the park. The people he put on the show had to be ready, he maintained. They had to be prepared for the break when it came.

When your moment comes, will you be ready?

Make no mistake, luck is and always will be a factor in success. Maybe 1 percent. But 99 percent of winning—finishing—will always come down to preparation, determination, and effort.

FOCUS, FOCUS, FOCUS

—

Maintaining focus is never more important
than when you can see the summit.

I had reached one of the lowest moments of my career. We hadn't been in North Carolina very long, about sixteen months. Although we were building a strong team, I was running out of money. The team hadn't matured enough to produce enough for me to continue to cover the expenses of our fast-growing organization, and I was tapped out. Right at this critical moment Bob Turley, my manager, called to tell me he was holding an emergency senior management retreat in Big Canoe, Georgia, about 240 miles away. I wasn't excited at all about this idea and I told him, "Bob, I'm broke. I don't have money for gas."

Always the great listener, he ignored my protest. "Listen, Art and Angela"—Art Williams, the president of the company, and his wife—"are giving up one of their few days off to come meet with the team. They're primarily doing it to make a last stab at saving your career. You have to come. If you get down here I'll give you fifty bucks to get back home. I don't care if you have to rob a bank to get the money. Figure it out." He actually said that. My bank robbing skills being what they were, I had to find another way. I can't remember how I found the money, but I did.

When Art showed up, he started by writing the two things you have to do to become a great leader on a piece of poster board. On one side he wrote in big letters GOOD PERSON. He explained exactly what he meant. You have *got* to be somebody people can trust. You have to be ethical, consistent, and reliable. If you say you're going to do something, you've got to do it. If you don't keep your commitments, people won't follow you.

Then he flipped the poster board over and wrote GOOD PRODUCER. Again he explained. Until you put *points on the board* and actually accomplish things there's no way to separate you from all the people that just talk a good game. And obviously the world is full of those people. Just by becoming a person who gets things done, you stand out.

He talked about these two points awhile and then paused, looked at me, and said, "Larry, you are not money motivated."

Now, I thought I'd just gotten the greatest compliment of

my life. I had been raised in the church. I wanted to live a life of service, to help people. My belief was you do the right things long enough, and surely goodness and mercy will follow—and money would rain down from the sky. When Art said I wasn't money motivated, I thought, "Wow, I'm so glad my selfless nature has stood out and that I can be recognized in such a wonderful way." It was like I'd won an Academy Award or something.

I said, "Well, thank you, Art, I've always tried to approach things that way."

In his response, he wasn't crude, but what I heard was, "No, stupid, you're *supposed* to be money motivated." Talk about a slap in the face! He then told me that if you're in business, you're supposed to make money—the purpose of business is to *produce* profit. The number-one reason people follow you or work for you is to earn an income. As the leader of your team and your business, if you're not money motivated—not focused on producing profit—none of them will make any money. Their greatest priority isn't a priority for you. "The last thing they need from you is more training on how to starve to death," he said.

The more I thought about it, the more I realized that when you are not focused on the bottom line—whatever the result is you need to win—you aren't focused on the right things, day-to-day, that will produce the right result. In business building, that result is financials: revenue and profit. In your career, it might be the quality of your work or the success of your strategies or the level of service you provide. All of these things impact the balance sheet, but you have to determine the most critical, bottom-line outcome that you need to produce in order to reach your career goals.

When you're close to achieving a big goal, it can be easy to lose focus. You're tired, you're struggling, you're doubting. And you may already be thinking ahead to the next big thing, overlooking the fact that you haven't finished *this* big thing.

When I met with Art that weekend, I had been in the business for a little over four years and was averaging about $3,000 or $4,000 a month. That wasn't enough to even cover my living and business expenses. I returned home (on Bob's $50) and immediately made some changes. I got our team organized around numbers. We established specific targets for every person on the team. We used the numbers to stir up competition. I stopped asking, "How are things going?" (To which the best producers and the worst producers always replied "Great!") Instead, I asked, "What are your numbers for the month?" I wanted to establish a new culture. I didn't turn into a tyrant. I just started asking the right questions. Immediately everyone got focused and stayed focus on producing. We started running a real business and working with purpose. As a result, we saw success at all levels.

What did it mean for me? It saved my business. Over the next few months, my monthly income jumped to $6,000, and then to $11,000, and then to $22,000. Obviously, on a personal level, this was great. I was finally producing results for the company and I was finally achieving my own goals for building a successful business and being able to provide a good life for my family. I was finally winning after struggling for so long.

The results for the team were equally meaningful. I was able to create an environment in which great things were happening to the team as a whole *and* people were growing their incomes and getting promotions. The growth came fast, too. A few months after that meeting, we promoted our top person to run his own office. His first month out he was paid $25,000. Over time, I helped hundreds of people build successful, six-figure businesses. They all had to do the work, but I was able to provide an environment that helped them focus on learning and doing the right things. None of that would have happened if I hadn't become focused on making the right things happen—the things that would get us over the finish line, month after month.

Winners win by staying focused on the right things until the job gets done.

DO THE MOST IMPORTANT THINGS

It's easy to waste time and resources when you're pushing toward a big goal. You're working hard, running in all directions, grinding yourself to a nub. But if you aren't focused, you probably aren't doing the most important things—the things that will get you to your goal. Shakespeare's famous line from *Macbeth*, "sound and fury, signifying nothing," comes to mind. Then when the money doesn't come in or you don't get the promotion, you're confused and frustrated and upset. And then the blaming and excuse-making start. Except for death and taxes, the one other sure thing in life is that a loser will never blame himself. It's got to be his teacher, his boss, his parents, his wife—someone, anyone but him.

When we lose, we lose by degrees. We get sidetracked by one thing and then another and before we know it, we're way off course. When we're close to finishing, we usually face a multitude of loose ends and new opportunities, and it can be easy to lose sight of the big goal. When we get bogged down in the minutia, we become inefficient. When we get excited about a new opportunity, we take our eye off the ball and become ineffective. To finish, we have to fight this tendency and focus. We have to avoid what Charles Hummel dubbed "the tyranny of the urgent." (You can still get copies of Hummel's original essay from 1967 by the same name.) "Concentrate all your thoughts upon the work at hand," said

Alexander Graham Bell. "The sun's rays do not burn until brought to a focus."

The most important thing is to keep the most important thing the most important thing.

Doing anything great will be inconvenient. It will require sacrifices. You'll have to ignore interesting or exciting things in your environment. You'll have to make changes to cross the finish line. You'll have to give up some of your current activities. In life we have a limited supply of money and time, and you have to trade them for the things you really want. You have to prioritize, because everything comes with a price. You'll have to make tradeoffs, and some will be tough. You'll have to eliminate some things you really enjoy from your schedule. Some of those sacrifices will be short-term, though.

There's got to be some element of "out with the old" before we achieve "in with the new." You're the one making the decisions. You can't be weak when tossing out the time and resource wasters. This is the time to take charge and remind yourself of the principles you've heard all your life:

- You can't be all things to all people all the time.

- You can't please all the people all the time, including yourself.

And if you can't get yourself to make those choices—to deny yourself some fun now for the bigger payoff later—you'll never be focused enough to finish the most important things well.

KICK OUT THE CLUTTER

Nick Saban is one of the best college football coaches in the game today. He's done the impossible at the University of Alabama—he's proven that he's good enough to stand alongside legendary coach Bear Bryant. And he's coached the team to three BCS national championships in four years.

He wins a lot. As a result, everything he does is scrutinized. One habit that has mystified reporters and team fans is Saban's dietary choices. He eats the same thing for breakfast and lunch *every day*. Yep, every day. Two Little Debbie Oatmeal Creme Pies for breakfast and a salad with either turkey or chicken for lunch. Why? According to an intensive profile in *GQ*, it "saves him the time of deciding what to eat each day and speaks to a broader tendency to habituate his behaviors."[18] He's found that the more he can take the thinking out of the things he's got to do over and over every day, the more time he saves for more important things. What does his lunch meal really matter, as long as he's getting some nutrition to keep him going? After the season is over he can look at the menu and order something tasty.

Do everything you can to free yourself up to focus on your priority.

Don't let clutter distract you. There are all sorts of clutter in life: mental, emotional, physical. Whatever kind you've got hanging around, find a way to get rid of it. It crowds out more important things.

You will always have restrictions on your time, energy, and other resources. You must say no to some things in order to focus on others. Make sure you're saying no to the unproductive things and yes to the most productive things. Spend the majority of your time on the things you most want to do (because they are likely the best use of your time) and get brutally efficient at everything else.

TAKE THE NO-PARACHUTE APPROACH

What's the no-parachute approach? I first heard the term "no-parachute person" from a speaker, Bill Glass, who presented to our high-school football team. He said that when you make a decision, you have to stick with it. And if you don't bring a parachute, you don't have a choice.

A winner knows how to commit. Before the plane takes off or the decision is made, a winner is gathering information, debating, and analyzing all the choices. Eventually the time comes to make a decision and once that decision is made they commit to the finish. They don't give themselves alternatives. They don't even consider the "excuse for failure" parachute. They're all in. They're obsessed. Finishing is the only option.

In the last chapter I wrote about adapting and making adjustments. When you're in the 2-percent zone, you might make minor adjustments to resolve last-minute problems. But this is not the time to make major adjustments—to rethink your course, to consider completely different goals. That time has passed. This is the time to focus and finish. You stick with it because the return on finishing is worth it, even if you think you might want to change course eventually. You don't quit college when you're in your last semester just because you aren't sure what you might do with your major. You don't shut down your new business the day before you open because you come up with a different business idea. You finish what you've started and *then* you figure out your next move.

Once you're in the 2-percent zone, anything other than finishing is just an excuse.

And if you're settling for excuses, you aren't committed. On an episode of *Shark Tank* last year, Mark Cuban told a young woman that he couldn't invest in her business because she didn't believe in it enough to overcome her own inhibitions and weaknesses. She had invested several years and a lot of money into it. She had a great product. But she wasn't selling anything.

Here was her excuse: She was an introvert. She found it difficult to promote the product, to call buyers who might put it in their stores. She was using her personality as an excuse for lack of growth. Really, she just wasn't pushing herself out of her comfort zone.

She seemed committed, but she wasn't really. Cuban essentially told her that if she wanted it enough, she wouldn't be making excuses for her weaknesses. She wasn't committed enough to try anything to win. What an indictment! He told her if she didn't believe in herself and product any more than that, there was no reason for him to invest. His comments stung, but even she knew he was right.

Face it, if you aren't committed enough to the opportunity to break through your personal barriers, to move past your comfort zone, to let go of your safety net, you'll never win. And if you aren't that committed, why should people take you seriously? Why should they buy from you? Why should they listen to your opinion and ideas, much less invest in you? The answer is they shouldn't. If you don't believe in you, why should anyone else? Your effort reveals how committed you are, and everyone can see it.

If you're still looking for excuses rather than answers, you may think you're committed, but you aren't. Somewhere in your thinking you've got a parachute—very likely an excuse—that you're counting on to carry you safely away from the hard work of winning. Until you get rid of the parachute, you won't have the commitment you need to finish.

* * *

If you want the reward, you have to go the distance. You have to keep fighting until you win. *You have to impose your will until you find success.* Whatever you want out of life, you must go through a process to get it. The process will take time, energy, determination, sacrifice, and relentless focus. If you want it enough, you'll find a way to get it done.

That's the mark of a winner. That's what makes winners stand out from the rest.

CHAPTER 5

DON'T SETTLE, KEEP IMPROVING

Ah, the one-hit wonders. We all know them. Music seems to be where they really shine, but you can see them in all walks of life. Entrepreneurs who were successful once, but never got another start-up running. The young shining stars in a company who start to fade after they rise to a certain position. Salespeople who shoot up the charts for a month or even a year and then drop out of sight. Where did they come from? Where did they go?

Being a one-hit wonder isn't necessarily a bad thing. The one-hit wonders of the world have achieved more than most. But wouldn't it have been great if they could have done it again . . . and again and again? What if Sam Walton stood in front of his first successful store in Rogers, Arkansas, in 1962 and said, "This is great. This is exactly what I was hoping for. We'll just keep this running, because one store is really all we need." What if Steve Jobs had stopped after the first Apple computer went to market? Think of the staggering opportunity that would have been lost.

Many people never get the momentum that comes with a big win. And many who do get it squander it. They fall into the same mental trap that keeps some people from winning at all: They have focused so hard for so long that when the win comes, they believe that more success will naturally follow. So they let up on the accelerator. They start to slow down. At first, they don't even notice. By the time they do, they're on a steady deceleration that leads to mediocrity. You might think that once you've won something big in life—the big assignment, the big promotion, the big raise, the big championship—you'd be past the mediocrity trap. No.

Winning the first time or first few times opens your eyes and explodes your confidence. You understand what winning requires, you know where you struggled, and you see lots of things you could improve the next time around. But unless you act on that newfound insight and energy, you'll start to slide backward. In life, you progress or you regress. The exciting breakthrough you worked so hard to achieve *is* exciting—for a while. But eventually it will become familiar and stale. Wanting more progress—to achieve something more, something new, something bigger—isn't greed, it's life.

Serial winners capitalize on the momentum of success.

They use it as a springboard for the next big thing and a series of bigger and bigger goals. They focus on winning long-term, not just in the short-term. As soon as they complete something or achieve a certain kind of success (sometimes even before), they immediately set their sights on the next goal, the next fulfilling experience, the next summit. It will bring them closer to their long-term vision and it will be bigger than the last win. Why? They know that

- greatness isn't winning once, it's winning consistently, and

- the best life is a life of challenge and growth.

I said it at the start of the book: Winning isn't a one-time thing, it's an all-the-time thing. It's not something you have to limit to one area of your life. It's an approach to everything in life. And it's not something you keep for yourself. It's something you can share with everyone around you.

Winners are constant works in progress. They are always

fighting for improvement. The only way to stay ahead of the crowd is to keep moving forward. Winning isn't about achieving a pinnacle of perfection, because it's never final. It's about growing, learning, taking risks, and being open to new ideas and opportunities.

Serial winners don't take their success for granted. They don't believe that they've "arrived." They're very aware of what they haven't yet achieved. Sure, they pause long enough to appreciate each win and to prepare for the next big push. But their progress motivates them to keep going; it doesn't convince them that it's finally time to slack off or pull back.

If you stop for too long, you'll have to overcome inertia all over again. Stopping and starting wears you down unnecessarily. You become less efficient. That's why the military fuels planes in the air. When you maintain your momentum you can travel farther. "Use it or lose it" is an important principle in life. Muscles, when neglected, start to shrivel. Cars, when they aren't driven, start to rust. A knife that isn't sharpened regularly becomes dull. When you win you sharpen your knife. You're efficient. You think quickly. You're disciplined. You are fine-tuned. When you slack off, all those advantages start to fade away. You lose your edge.

That's what separates serial winners. They don't let themselves go stale. They continue to improve so that they can win consistently—and achieve a lot more of the things they want to achieve. They like the winning approach to life and they never want to lose it.

THE ABI PRINCIPLE

—

If you've been waiting for the big secret,

the magic pill, the difference maker, here it is.

Throughout this book, I've been explaining the cycle of winning. Anybody can use most of the cycle—decide, overdo, adjust, finish—to win once or occasionally. But this book is about serial winners—people who win consistently. The big mystery for many people is how do they do it? How do some people move from one success to another? Sure, they stumble along the way. But they are back up and winning fast. How? I hear this question at least once a week. Here's the answer:

Always be improving.

Every other part of the winning cycle is important, but the ABI Principle (always be improving) is *the difference* between winning occasionally and winning consistently. It is *the difference* between serial winners and everybody else. It defines their approach to their careers, their hobbies, their relationships— to life.

Andy Young, a member of my team at Primerica who has achieved amazing success in the industry, can attest to the value of improving. When he was six years old, Andy's mother, a world-class musician, enrolled him in piano lessons. He spent hours practicing scales and arpeggios on the piano, becoming an accomplished pianist. Piano wasn't enough, though. He also began playing the tuba in the school band.

In high school, he become a grade 6 tuba player, the highest level of play one can achieve at that age. At the same time—and *nobody* does this—Andy quickly moved into a starting position on his football team, becoming captain after just one year. Again, he invested hours and hours in repetitive drills, pounding in the fundamentals he needed to become a champion defensive tackle. He even worked with one of the top strength trainers in the nation, Mike Mentzer, who happened to live nearby. Excellence in piano, tuba, and on the football field—all while maintaining his studies. The result? Andy had the pick of just about any free-ride football scholarship he wanted when he graduated.

While playing for Wake Forest University, Andy suffered several knee injuries and ended up being redshirted his senior year. Knowing Wake Forest would pay for his fifth year of college, Andy added a second major in Spanish. Again, he used continuous repetition to learn a new language in less than one year and ended up running the Wake Forest language lab as a result. When he graduated, Wachovia Bank put Andy to work as a translator in Bogotá, Columbia. He was that good, that fast.

No, Andy wasn't simply naturally talented—in *everything*. He just learned the methods of improving (and improving quickly!) and he applied them over and over again. Confidence in his ability to improve gave him faith in his ability to excel at almost anything.

ANYBODY CAN BECOME GREAT AT ALMOST ANYTHING

Andy has what is called a "growth mindset." Carol Dweck, a renowned psychologist, Stanford University professor, and researcher into why people succeed, puts people into two categories: growth mindset or fixed mindset. People with a fixed mindset believe that they are either smart or not, creative or not, talented in any given area or not. To succeed, they simply have to prove their strengths to the world. People with a growth mindset believe that effort can lead to improvement, that they can grow their skills and abilities. Guess which one produces long-term success and happiness in life?

You can always improve. Always! No matter what you want to do, no matter how far away you feel you are from a goal (within reason, of course), if you're willing to work for it, you can do it. The guarantee of the ABI Principle is that you can put it to work in any area of your life and make great progress. And the more you grow, the more you're capable of growing. Growth becomes a skill, and it can create exponential change in your life. As soon as you grow in one area, other areas that need attention become obvious. Improvement becomes as much a habit as eating and sleeping. And this is how winners transform themselves throughout their lives.

Serial winners recognize that improving in any area is like developing muscle. You don't go to the gym, work out one time with minimal effort or focus, and suddenly have a bodybuilder physique. No. You start, and you're terrible for a while. But you keep at it. Eventually, gradually, step by step, you get better. You improve. What seemed hard yesterday doesn't seem so hard today. You take it to the next level. You get good. Eventually, much of what you had to work to learn is second nature. It's obvious, right? Of course it is. You've done it before. You've been doing it your entire life. It's how you've learned everything.

What many people don't consider, though, is the other piece of improvement: judgment and instinct. A ten-cent word for it is heuristics. A heuristic is a rule-of-thumb mental short-cut. It forms in our brains as a result of repeated experiences. We rely on heuristics to make quick decisions, make quick judgments, and find quick solutions. I think of a heuristic as an educated instinct that you develop over time by learning and problem-solving. The more we work to improve and the more big goals we set, the more experiences we have that create these mental shortcuts that allow us to recognize patterns and move forward quickly and efficiently—either dodging bullets or pursuing winning opportunities. The better our judgment, the more losing situations we'll avoid and the more winning situations we'll pursue.

This is what the progression looks like:

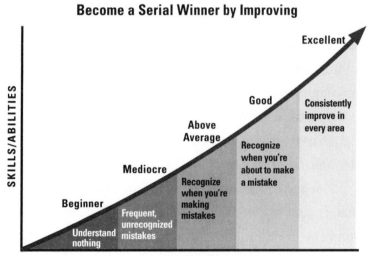

Become a Serial Winner by Improving

Once you master the basics, you can start making refinements. Once you're up to operational speed, you can start trusting your instincts more.

Develop a Winning Instinct

When I was learning to ride horses competitively, it took me a long time to recognize my mistakes. For instance, before you ride into the main ring, you warm up the horse. You're trying to work out your own nerves and get the horse limber so it can jump. When you start the warm-up, the rails are low. You want the horse to relax and loosen up gradually. In a few minutes he's going to be in the ring running and jumping at breakneck speed and you don't need for him to turn into a nervous wreck before he even starts. Slowly, step by step the rails are raised until you're up to five-foot jumps. But you've done it progressively and the horse doesn't think any of this is a big deal. Unless you've got a rookie rider running the show.

In my first few competitions, the trainers would yell at me, "Stop gigging him in the mouth! Stop jerking his head!" And I would be thinking, "What are they talking about? I'm not doing that, my hands are relaxed!" They would keep yelling louder and I'd keep getting madder until eventually, I would look down and see that instead of being relaxed and smooth, my hands were white-knuckled on the reins and I was violently yanking the horse's mouth down and back as we approached each fence. As you might imagine, that makes it very difficult for a horse to jump. I was so focused on galloping up to the first fence, I had no idea what my hands were doing. On the outside I tried to look calm and collected but my hands were in full panic mode. I was fooling no one, especially not the horse. It took a lot of practice before I could tell when I was doing it before the trainers yelled at me about it and a lot more before my hands naturally held the right position. (Don't feel too bad for the horse. He got me back by throwing me to the ground plenty of times.) It took a long time, but eventually I improved so much I was able to finish first in a competition out of a class of 110, including professionals and Olympic riders. Of course it was a training division and the fences weren't that high, but the former Mr. Spastic rider won.

Improving always begins with internalizing the fundamentals. You can't decorate a cake until it comes out of the oven. You have to bake the foundational knowledge into how you work. Over time your instincts will improve. Then your choices will begin to improve. You'll never get good enough to predict the future but you'll be making a lot more wise choices than foolish ones. And eventually you'll develop a winning instinct.

Serial winners see winning and losing patterns everywhere— in conversations, in people, in situations, in opportunities.

They're buried in the fabric of life. Winners have the eyes to see and the ears to hear. They know what to look for and what to listen for—because they have worked long and hard to open their eyes and ears. Consequently, they make better choices and win more consistently.

It's almost impossible to accomplish big things if you don't know what to look for and if you can't interpret what you're seeing. To succeed in any environment, you need to be able to spot the patterns that will turn out well and the patterns that are doomed to fail. It's an insane advantage. You'll pay a big price to develop it but it's the advantage that keeps on giving. You can use it the rest of your life. And because winners always want to accomplish something new and something bigger, they constantly fight to develop that advantage—to improve both their abilities and their judgment.

What to Improve and When

When is the best time to spot areas for improvement? When you're coming off of a great success. Serial winners take the time to consider the weaknesses, the flaws, and the imperfections. They know where they struggled the most when trying to finish the last big goal. Those struggles are opportunities for improvement. The farther away from that success you get, the less you remember those tough moments. You lose critical insight.

Watch people who aren't consistently successful. When

they finish a big project or achieve a goal, what do they do? They celebrate. "We did it! We won!" And they ignore the cracks in the armor that almost kept them from winning.

The best companies do project debriefs after they finish a big initiative or finish work for a client. What went well? What didn't? What should we do more of next time? Where can we improve? Companies that will never be great don't do this, usually because they're afraid to answer these questions. They don't want to admit that they could have done some things better. If they do, the next obvious question is, "What are we going to do about it?" And they don't want to invest the time, effort, or money in developing better systems, better talent, or better leadership.

What should you try to improve? I can't answer that. Only you are living your life. Only you know the areas of greatest stress, so only you know where the opportunities for improvement exist. Find one. Start working on it now. Start planning how you're going to win faster next time.

KEEP THE FUN COMING

The joy of doing new and bigger and better things never fades, because no matter what you've accomplished and no matter how old you are, learning, improving, and new adventures are the key to an exciting life.

A new play opened at an Off Broadway theater about the time I was working on this chapter. *Billy & Ray* tells the story of director and screenwriter Billy Wilder and author Raymond Chandler developing the screenplay for *Double Indemnity*. The director of the play happens to be Garry Marshall, the legendary actor, director, writer, and producer behind hits *Happy Days*, *The Odd Couple*, *Pretty Woman*, *Beaches*, etcetera, etcetera. Marshall has done a bit of theater before; it's not a big surprise that he's trying his hand at it again. But this play is different. It's an exploration of a contentious relationship between two big-ego artists, one a recovering alcoholic, trying to get around the censors who were charged with enforcing the Hollywood Production Code of the 1940s. The novel they were adapting was steamy and violent. Not an easy job, especially for two people who, as the rumors go, were in constant battle. But eventually, *Double Indemnity* launched the film noir genre.

And that's what makes this a new adventure for Marshall. "This was part of the beginning of film noir, and I'm known for doing film blanc," he told the Associated Press. "This was my adventure into another genre. It's always good to be challenged and see something new."[19] In a TV interview I watched, he talked about the new opportunities it presented, the new people he met, the friends he made. And while he talked, you could see the sparkle in his eye.

This type of move—to try something different—isn't that uncommon for creative, driven people. But Garry Marshall is eighty years old! What do you think you'll be doing when you're eighty? Trying something completely new? What about ten years from now? Or how about next year? Why not? Why not you?

There are lots of people Marshall's age who simply wouldn't be trying anymore. They wouldn't be interested in learning something new, trying something new, meeting new people. Heck, there are people half his age who already think like that. They're done. They've checked out. You hear them say things like, "It's time I started enjoying my life" or "I'm ready for a little stability" or "If I can get to this point, I'm going to kick back and unplug." It's great to have balance, stability, and leisure time, but that can quickly and easily turn into boring, routine, stale, and cynical.

Being energized about life, having that sparkle in your eye . . . it doesn't happen all by itself. It comes from an attitude of refusing to stagnate, of seeking out new ideas and new experiences, of seeking positive change in your life. What adds value and enjoyment and fulfillment are new relationships, new challenges, new experiences, and new levels of productivity. Winners stay plugged in.

Do you lead an enjoyable, fulfilling, satisfying life from minute to minute, week to week, year to year? If not, you aren't doing enough new things. You aren't injecting energy into your life. You need to get that sparkle back in your eye. Because you know what they say: the eyes are the windows to the soul.

Serial winners know that the excitement of life is found in the question, "What's next?" They continue to move forward.

They challenge themselves, meet new people, learn new things, and improve. As a result, they stay fresh, stimulated, energized, and productive.

Life is action and change.
You don't have to stop until you die.

If you feel drained by life, or that you're just going through the motions, it's time to use the ABI (always be improving) Principle to take control. Have you ever thought about living somewhere else? Have you ever thought about a job or even a career change? Do you need to invest more energy in your personal relationships so that they're more fulfilling, for you and others? Look at the areas of your life where you feel stuck or stale and start empowering yourself to make positive change. Every improvement will shoot a jolt of positive electricity and excitement into your world.

GROWTH BY DEGREES

—

How do we improve?

Little by little.

All real growth comes by degrees. It's your only option when you want things to get better. It's how people become champions. It's how businesses grow. It's how great books are written. It's how zeroes become heroes. Gradually, over time.

We're all lousy in the beginning. Whenever we start out on some new course, we won't be any good. Every project was a lost cause at some point. Every MVP was a dud at some point. Every movie was a bomb at some point. The first day at a new job, you'll be awkward. The first time you try to speak a new language, you'll sound awful. So what? It's true of everybody.

Serial winners don't run from the awkwardness or grinding effort of growth. They embrace it.

They grind to get ready to compete and they grind while competing. It's how they transform themselves to elite performance. It may not always be fun, but it leads to the fun of winning.

To take the risk of doing something exciting, something new, you have to be willing to start at the bottom. You have to be willing to be lousy for a while. You have to be willing to swallow your pride and get back to work. And you have to have the patience and faith required to gradually internalize what you are learning, for it to become a way of life.

Winners use four methods to stay motivated and to keep moving forward in their growth:

- measurement and competition,

- learning from those who have already won,

- putting their own twist on it, and

- working better.

USE MEASUREMENT AND COMPETITION

How do you know how valuable something is? If somebody says to you, "This movie is great!" how do you know if it's true? If you're trying to judge how good you are at something, how do you do it?

Value is established by comparison.

Without a standard to which we can hold ourselves, we have no way of knowing whether we're improving or not. What are goals? They are standards of measurement that we set for ourselves—a way to judge our performance and determine the need for improvement. Study after study has shown that we are happiest and that we excel when we have a way to judge our progress. The best runners want to be in the lane next to the toughest competition. They know they'll be driven to run faster if they are. And if they're going to lose, they want to see how much they need to improve to beat the best runner next time.

Winners like reality. They want to know the facts. They like numbers. They want to figure out how to get ahead. They aren't worried about the effort, they just want to identify what it will take. Losers hate numbers. They would prefer to be vague. They don't want to commit themselves. They

want a lot of weasel room so when they miss their target
people aren't as likely to notice.

Back before farmers had big machines that could be run by
one person and pick up all the cotton for thousands of acres,
you had to go out and pick cotton by hand. My Uncle Martin
had cotton fields and when the crop was ready, he would have
to get that cotton in fast. It was an all-hands operation. He
would go out into the community and pick up any farmhands
he could find, but every member of the family would be in the
fields too. When I was very young, if we were visiting, I would
be out there. Even my sixty-year-old grandmother would be
out there. We would head into the fields early in the morning
and pick cotton all day long.

Now, Uncle Martin may have been a farmer, but he knew
more about managing for performance than a lot of the corporate executives I've met in life. Everybody got paid for what
they picked, but to make sure he got the best performance out
of each one of us, Uncle Martin would give everybody a goal
based on what we were capable of. The little kids might get a
goal of twenty-five pounds, while the biggest guys would get
a goal of 200 pounds. At the end of the day, if you picked your
goal you would get an ice cold RC Cola and a MoonPie. If
you've never had either of these fantastic refreshments, I sug-
gest you go out and find them now. Let me tell you, after a hot
day in the sun in South Georgia, it was a bonus worth fighting for. If you didn't hit your goal, you had to sit in the back
of the truck and watch everybody else enjoy their RC Colas

and MoonPies. Toward the end of the day, people would come in to have their bags weighed. You'd know if anyone came up short because they would immediately grab their bags and run out to the field to get those last few pounds picked—there was no way they were going to miss out on their RC Cola and MoonPie. Uncle Martin knew how to motivate.

If you don't measure yourself, it's easy to fall short of your full potential. You'll just keep doing the same thing over and over, without making real progress. When you have a goal that's just a bit beyond your reach or past performance, you push yourself just a bit harder, and that's how you improve. On the other hand, activity or practice without a serious effort to improve will result in no improvement at all.

Measurement Helps Us Focus

If you can believe it, until the 1980s, most people, including scientists, thought that excellence was primarily a result of genetics. There's a long history of belief in the myth of natural talent.

Even though the idea "practice makes perfect" has been around for hundreds of years, in the late 1980s and early 1990s, researchers began to prove that "the effect of practice on performance is larger than earlier believed possible."[20] Um . . . duh! The real breakthrough, though was that not just any practice was enough. Only deliberate practice—practice that is specifically focused on improvement, not just going through the motions—leads to growth. And having a way to measure your performance or progress is a key component of that type of practice.

You need a goal that requires focused effort because it's slightly beyond your capabilities and you need immediate or quick feedback on how you're performing related to that goal. Researchers have shown that these pieces are critical for maintaining your motivation when you're trying to improve.

Good things don't come out of halfhearted actions.

As we get better and better, we're more likely to achieve a state of flow in some of the activities or work we do. Flow was first described by psychologist Mihaly Csikszentmihalyi and his team of researchers. It's another word for "the zone." We enter into it when we become so engrossed in an activity that it consumes every bit of our attention. The research found that people who regularly achieve flow are happier and more content in life. It's also a state critical for high performance. What are the necessary conditions? You need a clear set of goals, a way to get regular and immediate feedback on your progress, and the perception that the goal is a challenge, but still within your abilities.

Set goals for your improvement. Give yourself a standard of measurement. And then watch how fast you surpass it!

Competition Helps Drive Us

Winners aren't afraid of competition. In fact, most of them love it. They seek it out. They know it drives them to their best effort. It introduces challenges that force them to focus. It drives them to break through plateaus, to be creative in how they solve problems, to innovate. It keeps them fresh, learning new things and getting better at the things they already know how to do. It makes them more efficient. Guess what? Their performance goes through the roof.

Sometimes, we're competing against ourselves—trying to beat our best performance. Sometimes we're competing against others—in sales competitions, for promotions, against other companies in the market. Regardless, when we compete, we learn something about ourselves and the world in which we're operating. We put our ideas and skills to work. And we make progress.

When we stop competing in life and when we stop measuring ourselves, we stop improving. We lose our edge and our energy. We grow stale.

LEARN FROM PEOPLE WHO
HAVE ACTUALLY WON

When I see people struggling to improve, it's usually for one of two reasons. The first is that they're turning to false prophets—people who haven't actually won, or haven't won big, but talk a good game—for guidance. The second is that they're afraid to align themselves with winners. They're afraid of the comparison. They're intimidated.

This is loser thinking.

At some point in my life, I decided I wanted to learn how to ski. As a family, we had skied a few times and I enjoyed it. But I was tired of learning in fits and starts, and I wanted to be able to ski on the big mountains. I decided I would find the best teacher I could find and spend a week learning everything I could. That teacher was Phil Mahre, one of the greats in the sport. He's a three-time FIS Alpine Ski World Cup winner and has won gold and silver Olympic medals. He and his twin brother, Steve, opened the Mahre Training Center in Keystone, Colorado in 1985. They won gold and silver for giant slalom in the 1984 Olympics. It seemed like the right place to learn.

The camp was divided into groups and one morning our group had Phil all to ourselves. What a thrill it was to ask him our questions. He didn't say a whole lot more than we had already heard from the other instructors, but I noticed that each answer was a little more detailed, a little more precise. As he talked it became obvious why he had been able to win a gold medal when no other American had been able to do it before him. He understood the nuances just a little better.

While the rest of us took forever finding the right boots ands skis, it was obvious you could have strapped two-by-fours to his feet and it wouldn't have made any difference. He skied like a dream. You might think it was intimidating to ski down the slope with him, but it wasn't. I realized as I watched him that he looked so good because he had done it hundreds of thousands of times. I'd be an idiot to get depressed because I couldn't show up and ski like him three days later. He'd been skiing for over twenty years. He literally grew up on a mountain. His father was the mountain manager of White Pass ski resort in Washington. By the time Phil and his brother were twelve, ski manufacturers were sending them free skis. And Phil made it onto the US Ski Team at age fifteen. If I had been skiing for that long, I might look at least a little more like him going down the mountain. But I hadn't, so why should I expect to be anything like him?

Most important, though, is that by learning from him rather than being intimidated by him, I gained valuable insights that helped speed up my learning process.

Winners have already simplified and streamlined the process for doing whatever it is you're learning.

Why is it so important to learn from the best? They know how to win because they've paid the price. They've already put in the 10,000 hours we've heard it takes to achieve excellence. Along the way, they've innovated, they've solved problems the average performers haven't solved. When you learn from them, you'll acquire the fundamentals faster because they've already separated the important from the irrelevant. Proverbs 13:20 says it all: "He who walks with wise men will be wise, but the companion of fools will suffer harm."

If you want to always be improving, advice from those who have already been where you want to go can be priceless.

Be Open to Good Ideas from Any Source

Be careful, though. Don't be blind to what you can learn from people younger or less experienced than you, from colleagues, and from competitors. Life is always changing. We all have different experiences and the best performers, even the less experienced, are learning new things every day. Do you think surgeons refuse to read articles by people not long out of med school? Do you think winners in the tech industry don't pay attention to the ideas that students at MIT or Caltech are developing? Other people are figuring out how to improve the world just as you are. They should be learning from you. You should be learning from them. The process drives both of you higher. The important thing is to be open to new ideas, and to use your judgment as to whether they're winning ideas that have turned into big accomplishments. You aren't looking for untested theories.

Winning ideas are free. If it works for someone else, it can work for you. If you find one you like, try it out and see how far you can go with it.

Walt Disney built the Disney empire that way. He would constantly visit different departments, picking up exciting new ideas and stories everywhere he went. Then he would pass them along to the people in the next department he visited. It not only kept him stimulated, it kept his entire company buzzing and improving.

Put Yourself in a Position to Study Winners

When trying to learn from winners, it's important to choose the right environment. You need to be able to watch them perform. Don't rely on them to tell you what they do. Frankly, they usually can't. Few of us can accurately analyze and communicate exactly how we achieve what we achieve. When a master tells you his system for better parenting or a more effective exercise regimen or stronger sales, he's telling you what he thinks he does. He's telling you how he does it *from his perspective*. But he may be too close to the situation and he probably doesn't recognize how much of his success lies in something that's unique to him, something others simply can't copy. Also, you're interpreting everything you hear or read. The result is your interpretation of his interpretation of a personally successful system. This is why we usually struggle to achieve the same results that winners achieve when we try to apply their systems or methods *exactly*. Copying others, even the best in the world, will only get you started.

> *Fundamentals can be taught,*
> *but greatness must be caught.*

Spend as much time as possible with people who are already where you want to be. The intangibles of a winner's system—the attention to detail, how they think, and how they go about their business—are all keys to winning. Big success is found in the finer points of execution. The best way to pick those up is get close enough to see them operate. And the real fun and satisfaction comes when you start to use their ideas, make adjustments, and discover those finer points for yourself.

PUT YOUR TWIST ON IT

If you're working with robots, machines, and computers, one system for completing a task successfully will work. It's why millions or even billions of people use the same software or online service for writing or for managing email or for searching the Internet or for sharing information with "friends." One system meets most of our needs.

Human work is different—because human beings are different. The things each of us does to improve and succeed are based on a unique set of parameters—personality, experiences, preferred ways of learning and doing. We all have our own strengths, attitudes, skills, talents, opinions, relationships, and viewpoints.

Once you've mastered the fundamentals of anything, if you want to win big, you've got to put your own twist on them.

This is not something you need to force or obsess over. It will happen naturally if you don't make the rookie mistake of trying to copy every single thing you see your role model do. That works to get you started sometimes but as you pick up speed let your personality shine through. Why? Because winners innovate. After they master the fundamentals, they make what they learn their own. As they apply the fundamentals— as they *do* things—they develop their own ideas for improving. The subconscious starts sending suggestions for making things faster and better. And that process of innovation keeps them engaged.

Your greatest achievements will come from things you figure out for yourself, and you figure them out by doing, not
watching. Once you've got the fundamentals down, continu-
ing to obsess over your role model will simply lead you to
become a pale imitation of the original. Do you want to watch
golfers trying to imitate Tiger Woods's swing, or do you want
to watch Tiger Woods? Would you rather watch somebody
cover Eric Clapton's songs or Eric Clapton? What's more
valuable, an almost-perfect copy of a Picasso or the original
painting? Be original! If you want to become great, go beyond
the fundamentals you can learn from others and do something
special and unique.

When new ideas pop into your head, try them, don't ignore
them. If they work, keep them. If they don't, move on and try
something else. You find out what works for you by trying to
improve every area of your life. The things that work become
your personal algorithm for winning. It doesn't matter if it
works for anybody else. It doesn't matter if it makes sense to
anybody else. It only has to work for you. Organization is a
great example. Some people only keep an electronic calendar. Some people need a hard copy on their desk because they
need the visual reminder. Some people need a perfectly clean
desk at all times in order to get anything done. Some people
are inspired and motivated by a little clutter.

I have a friend, Bill, who carries a toothbrush and tooth-
paste everywhere he goes. Bill brushes his teeth after every
meal and after any snack. It might sound OCD to you, but for

him, it works. It's part of his algorithm and it's part of how he has maintained his success. He's always on top of his game, he's very consistent, he stays in shape, and he wins.

Your quirks are what make you *you*. Whatever your quirks, they are your way of establishing, "This is the way I'm going to live my life. I don't care what other people think. I don't care what comes at me." It allows you to maintain a structure for your life, discipline, and a sense of control—something we all need to feel stable in a constantly changing world. That sense of control helps us maintain a positive outlook, and research has shown that happiness leads to success rather than following it.[21] Happier people are more successful, across the board.

The key for you is to lock in on the things that attract and energize you. It's the way out of weakness to confidence and strength. You can improve yourself, but you've got to *be* yourself. When you're being yourself you're not acting, posing, or pretending. You're acting naturally, because only you know how to be you. When you're pretending to be someone else, you will always be an inferior version and you'll know it. Copying somebody implies that they are better and you are inferior. This mindset makes you insecure and vulnerable. You'll focus on the comparison, the negatives. As a result, you'll be weak, you'll be timid, and you'll be ineffective.

Somehow, you've gotten this far in life. You've built some experience. You've had some successes. You've learned some lessons. You've developed relationships. You've found you're pretty good at doing certain things. You've probably developed a substantial list of likes and dislikes. You know how you like to work. You know who you like to work with. You've spent your entire life becoming who you are today. Use what you've got and develop it into the things you need. How? The ABI Principle.

Ask yourself, "How am I going to do it? What's my plan? What's my system? What's going to work for me?" Answering these questions is the key to the highest level of improvement and to achieving big things.

STAY IN CONTROL OF YOUR TIME

Mediocrity sneaks up on unsuspecting winners by flooding them with new opportunities. They get distracted just enough, just slightly from doing the things that got them to the top. They lose what would seem to others an imperceptible amount of their intensity and focus. Before they realize it, they have lost their winning edge and they slump.

When you start to win, your life changes. You have more opportunities available to you. More people want you on their team or in their network, and more people want to be on your team and in your network. If your wins meant financial rewards, budgeting your money becomes less of an issue. The real focus becomes budgeting your time and energy. You have to be disciplined like never before. The penalty for getting off track is losing your focus on steady improvement, and that leads to short-lived victory.

Limit distractions and eliminate time wasters

Spend your time on improving and absorbing the new opportunities coming your way. Everyone has fat in his or her schedule. Not every activity is critical. Work to find ways to get the most out of your schedule. Things that take an hour can probably get done in thirty or forty-five minutes. Many of the things that you always did in the past could be delegated to others. Analyze how you are spending your time each day. Think about what is really important and weed out the unimportant. Make preparation a priority. Don't just keep doing the same things because you have always done them. Move on so you can move up.

Serial winners are good at saying no.

Nobody can do it all. And nobody expects you to sacrifice your health, well-being, or success by overloading yourself with obligations. Life is all about choices. Don't apologize for being disciplined and organized and don't let others tempt you into relaxing your commitment. Maintain the time and energy you need to focus on the work that will help you win. You don't have to be mean, but you do have to be definite. The inexperienced will want to say yes to everyone and everything, but soon they realize that doesn't work.

If you've won, you know how to work hard. The question is, are you working smart? Could you be working smarter? Look for ways to simplify and streamline. Look for ways to make maximum use of your precious time. How can you get the essentials done faster? How can you compress the timeline for your next win?

Finally, fight for stability in your personal life. When you're chasing goals, your life can seem chaotic. When you need to, call a time-out. Being disciplined doesn't mean devoting all your time and energy to your next goal and your next and your next. It means winning without sacrificing your health or the most important thing in life—your relationships with people. Remember, you need recovery time. Block out time to recharge personally, to stay healthy physically and mentally, and to devote quality time to the people in your life.

* * *

Winners race through the finish line and immediately set their sights on the next target. Why? Because improving is the key to growth and growth is the key to winning. You can't really count someone a winner who's only won once. What about all the other things they wanted to do in life? Real winning is developing a *winning approach to life*. A winning approach helps you stay positive and moving forward. It helps you bounce back from failure or catastrophes. It helps you maintain excitement and energy in your life. If you don't fight to improve, you won't have an answer for "What's next?"

It's not where you are that matters; what matters is where you're headed.

Raise your sights and get bigger goals. Don't take a chance on losing your hunger. Give yourself a solid reason to continue driving hard. It's great to win once, but when you continue to win you lead a completely different kind of life. Return to the fundamentals that got you to where you are now. Remind yourself that it's as hard to keep winning as it is to win the first time. Accept the challenge to stay on top.

BECOME A SERIAL WINNER

Not long before he died, I had the opportunity to have a long talk with Bob Turley about his eight years—and eight World Series wins—with the New York Yankees. He spent his life surrounded by winners in every world—sports, business, entertainment, politics. Every day he spent time in the field and in the dugout with people like Joe DiMaggio, Mickey Mantle, Yogi Berra, Whitey Ford, and all the other Yankee legends. He had spent time with seven different US presidents. I wanted his perspective on what makes the greats different from everybody else. Even though we had worked together for decades, his response still surprised me. This is what he told me:

- None of them really thought they were that good. They generally were a humble lot.

- Every day they worked at improving (probably because they didn't think they were that good).

- They all absolutely loved what they were doing. It seemed they just loved it a little bit more than everybody else.

This book isn't a magic pill or a one-size-fits-all formula for winning, because everybody is different. Every life is different. Every situation is different. Most important, though, is that what you love isn't necessarily what I love. And vice versa. If we want to be great at what we love, all we can do is look at the patterns that play out consistently in the lives of people who seem to get it right.

If you watch long enough and look close enough, what you discover is a cycle. The cycle leads to win after win, and it's made up of repeated action: *decide, overdo, adjust, finish, improve.*

We learned these fundamentals as kids. They aren't new, they aren't hard, but they require attention and focus.

I said in the introduction that this is a doing book—because that's the most basic truth about serial winners. They do things, and keep doing things. They don't mope, they don't wish, they don't wait, they don't hope. They want what they want too much to waste time and energy. They do the five things I've described over and over again, in their own way and to fulfill their own purposes.

So if this book isn't a magic pill, what is it? It's a guide to self-management. Self-management seems like a psychological issue—maintaining the right attitude and mindset. We're told over and over again that we should hire for attitude. The right attitude is the key to success. We need to adjust our attitude. Attitude is everything. Well, I think it's the reverse. The more we adjust what we do, the better our attitude. The more we stay on the winning cycle, the better our attitude. Because doing something—things that move you forward, productive things, tough things—helps us escape the dark, negative places. The cycle of winning is about positive, productive action, and it builds a positive, productive attitude. The only way to change your attitude is to change what you're doing. You need something to feel positive about.

Of course, there's an internal motivation factor we can't ignore. Why do some people have energy and others don't? Because they've got something they want to do. Going after the things we want—interesting things—is a drive we're born with.

Just watch how hard it is for a parent to distract a two-year-old from something he really wants. Following that drive is the key to exciting, rewarding lives. It's how we make an impact on the world—by making discoveries and sharing them.

Self-management is grounded in the desire and then the decision to make your life count, to accomplish big things, to make a big contribution to the world. And serial winners do, over and over again. They create a ripple of success that influences the people around them—the example they set, the things they talk about, where they focus their energy and time. Their influence compounds over time, the more they win. The foundation of that influence is love. They love what they do, they love making a difference, they love growing and improving, they love being able to inspire and help others, and most of all they just love living a life of achievement.

Sports Illustrated spent six months researching homeless high-school and college athletes. The stories they gathered are fascinating and heroic, but I thought one finding was especially interesting. As Jon Wertheim, Sports Illustrated executive editor, explained, "We assume it's aspirational, kids want to dunk, kids want to be Kevin Durant because he scores 30 points a game, and what we find is . . . a lot of kids really identify with what he had to overcome. Those back stories . . . [are] really internalized by an awful lot of kids."[22]

When you get yourself into a winning cycle, it's impossible for it not to impact everyone around you in a positive way. You don't have to be a sports superstar. You can have equally important and positive influence on your team and in your company, in your family and in your community. If we all live the richest life possible, it's personally fulfilling, but it also changes the world. That's why you don't want to be short-sighted and stop, before you've done the really big things you want to do and that you're capable of doing—the things God designed you to do.

Do you want to move up and make a bigger impact? If you do, now's the time because the clock is ticking. The world is full of people with good intentions who *almost* get around to them. What the world needs is more people who actually do things. That can be you. That needs to be you. Become a serial winner and make your world and the world around you a better place.

ACKNOWLEDGMENTS

I wrote this book because at some point I realized I had been the fortunate beneficiary of a fantastic amount of insight and wisdom from more than my fair share of serial winners. You can find many of their names in the pages of this book. The greatest honor I could think of was to share their words or tell their stories.

Formulating and refining ideas is a time-consuming and sometimes tedious process. For me, it wouldn't have been possible without an intelligent, hard-working, and most important, enthusiastic support team. In the early stages of this project, Venessa Sylvester and Tracy Stuever led the way and provided invaluable support. Susan O'Connell and Sean O'Connell also contributed valuable feedback. Over the past year, my assistant Taylor Hamlin's organizational and people skills have made it possible for things to stay on track and maintain forward momentum as Brent Cole and Lari Bishop worked with me to take the most important ideas that had emerged and hammer the book into its final shape.

I have also been surrounded by family, friends, and business associates who have helped me stay on the winning track and accomplish important things in my life. My two sons, Adam and Bryan, have always kept me on my toes and kept me honest. I'll never forget when my son, Adam, at eight, said to me, "Dad, excuses are like belly buttons. Everybody's got one." And Bryan never failed to remind me that the sky was the limit and to always go for the best things in life. For that, I am also grateful.

Through all my struggles and triumphs, my faith in Jesus Christ has guided me. Without it, I would not be the person I am and I would not have achieved what I have. I am thankful for it every second of every day. As far as I'm concerned, that's the ultimate secret to serial winning.

ENDNOTES

1. Lisa Blackwell, Kali Trzesniewski, and Carol Dweck, "Implicit Theories of Intelligence Predict Achievement Across an Adolescent Transition," *Child Development*, v. 78, n. 1, 2007, 246–263.

2. William Deresiewicz, *Excellent Sheep: The Miseducation of the American Elite and the Way to a Meaningful Life*, Free Press, 2014, 3.

3. This line was written for Tomlin by Jane Wagner and performed by Tomlin in *The Search for Signs of Intelligent Life in the Universe*.

4. Annika Sorenstam, "SwingFix: Think box drill" (video), Golfchannel.com.

5. Bent Flyvbjerg, Mette Skamris Holm, and Søren L. Buhl, "Underestimating Costs in Public Works Projects: Error or Lie?" *Journal of the American Planning Association*, v. 68, n. 3, 2002, 279–295.

6. Dorothy Carnegie, ed., *Dale Carnegie's Scrapbook: A Treasury of the Wisdom of the Ages*, Simon & Schuster, 1959. As quoted in "Tips for Success: 20 Tips for Overcoming Fear," Dalecarnegie.com (blog), June 5, 2009.

7. "Attendance, Adherence, Dropout, and Retention," PTDirect. com.

8. Michael Jordan with Rick Telander, "My First Time," *ESPN The Magazine* (online), May 28, 2001.

9. Associated Press, "Ryan Lochte Wins 400 IM in Blowout," ESPN.com, July 29, 2012.

10. Mark Bradley, "Falling for Richt," Inspire21.com, October 25, 2011.

11. Josh Kendall, "On-the-Job Training for Richt," OnlineAthens. com (*Athens Banner-Herald*), November 4, 2011.

12. Patrick Thean, *Rhythm: How to Achieve Breakthrough Execution and Accelerate Growth*, Greenleaf Book Group, 2014, 221.

13. Linda Tischler, "The Beauty of Simplicity," *Fast Company* (online), November 1, 2005.

14. Cameron Morfit, "With a Shot Only He Could Hit, Bubba Watson Wins Masters in Playoff," Golf.com, April 9, 2012 (updated December 1, 2014).

15. Matthew Cronin, *Epic: John McEnroe, Björn Borg, and the Greatest Tennis Season Ever*, John Wiley & Sons, 2011, 49.

16. Kevin Clark and Daniel Barbarisi, "Bill Belichick: The NFL's Scary Alex Trebek," *The Wall Street Journal* (online), January 14, 2015.

17. "The Start of Something Special," *A Football Life: Bill Parcells*, The NFL Network (available on NFL.com).

18. Warren St. John, "Nick Saban: Sympathy for the Devil," *GQ* (online), September 2013.

19. Associated Press, "Garry Marshall, Knight of Light, Goes Dark with 'Billy & Ray,'" SFGate.com, October 14, 2014.

20. K. Anders Ericsson, Ralf Th. Krampe, and Clemens Tesch-Römer, "The Role of Deliberate Practice in the Acquisition of Expert Performance," *Psychological Review*, v. 100, n. 3, 1993, 363.

21. Sonja Lyubomirsky, as quoted in "Review of Research Challenges Assumption that Success Makes People Happy: Happiness May Lead to Success via Positive Emotions," American Psychological Association press release, December 18, 2005. Available at www.apa.org.

22. John Wertheim and John Hockenberry, "Homeless Youths Find Safety Net in Sports," *The Takeaway*, NPR, October 28, 2014.

ABOUT THE AUTHOR

In the mid 1970s, Larry Weidel was just a few years out of college when he was promoted to a well-paying job as the supervisor for a top real-estate construction company in Atlanta, Georgia. However, it was not long before the oil embargo and economic turmoil hit the company hard, and Larry found himself without a job. He was forced to accept unemployment checks and food stamps in order to feed his young family. Refusing to settle just for any available job and determined to find a more stable industry, he decided to tough it out until he found the right opportunity. It took nine long months, but in 1975, he found it—a chance to help build A.L. Williams, now Primerica, an award-winning financial services company that has grown to more than 100,000 representatives.

During his decades at Primerica, Larry has learned the fundamentals of winning from mentors like Yankees baseball legend Robert "Bullet Bob" Turley and Art Williams, the founder of the company and a billionaire philanthropist. He has built a team that consistently outperforms. Over the years, hundreds of his sales and management team members have been able to generate six-figure annual incomes and even more have become millionaires.

Larry holds weekly coaching calls for an audience of hundreds of top leaders across the United States and Canada. His videos on leadership, sales, recruiting, and training are widely popular inside and outside the company. Through his website, WeidelonWinning.com, he shares articles, podcasts, and other resources to help people overcome the obstacles preventing them from winning in any area of life.

Larry is a proud graduate of Georgia Tech, and due to his success in business has been able follow the advice of his cousin H. Edward Roberts (the inventor of the first commercially available desktop computer) to "stay fresh and motivated by following his natural curiosity." This guidance has spurred him to try new and interesting things that also provide opportunities to spend quality time with his family. He plays guitar, banjo, and the drums; is an avid skier, golfer, and hunter; and today devotes much of his spare time to photography (you can see his work at larryweidelphotography.com). Pursuing the patterns of winning, even in his hobbies, has kept him energized and has exposed him to people and ideas that have profoundly influenced his business and his life.

He splits his time between Palm Beach, Florida, and Aspen, Colorado.

For more insights on winning and to download your copy of the **Serial Winner Workbook,** go to **WeidelonWinning.com.**

Follow Larry on Twitter—@LarryWeidel—for insights, articles, news, and more.